WATER-CONSERVING GARDENS *and* LANDSCAPES

Water-saving ideas

Plant selection list

Home drip irrigation guide

Easy-care landscapes

All-region zone maps

BY JOHN M. O'KEEFE

*A Down-to-Earth Gardening Book
from Storey Publishing*

Storey Communications, Inc.
Schoolhouse Road
Pownal, Vermont 05261

DEDICATION

To my father, Jack O'Keefe,
who left behind the dark coal mines of his youth
and built homes in the sunlight for thousands of families,
who taught me reverence for all living things,
and who, at 81 years of age, can still garden my socks off.

ACKNOWLEDGMENT

To my wife, Stephanie,
who had the idea for this book,
and to all the gardeners, nursery personnel,
landscape designers, and friends
who gave freely of their knowledge,
from Max at the hardware store
to Tom and Pat at the Newberry Feedstore & Nursery.

CONTENTS

Front and back cover photographs by Jerry Pavia
Cover designed by Carol Jessop
Text designed by Carol Jessop and Meredith Maker
Text produced by Meredith Maker
Illustrations by Alison Kolesar
Illustrations on pages 78 and 83 courtesy of Planetary Solutions
Edited by Constance L. Oxley
Indexed by Gail Damerow

Editor's note: The editor would like to thank Professor Henry W. Art
for all of his contributions to this book.

Chart on page 23 from *Stonescaping: A Guide to Using Stone in Your Garden*
by Jan Kowalczewski Whitner, Garden Way Publishing, 1992.
Regional Guide to Plant Selection on page 93 created by Professor Henry W. Art.
Some text selections from Ornamental Grasses on page 113 from *Successful
Perennial Gardening* by Lewis and Nancy Hill, Garden Way Publishing, 1988.

Printed in the United States by Capitol City Press
First printing, November 1992
Library of Congress Cataloging-in-Publication Data

O'Keefe, John M., 1935–
    Water-conserving gardens and landscapes / John M. O'Keefe.
        p.   cm. — (A Down-to-earth book)
    Includes bibliographical references and index.
    ISBN 0-88266-787-4 — ISBN 0-88266-786-6 (pbk.)
    1. Landscape gardening—Water conservation.   2. Trickle irrigation.   3.
Landscape gardening—United States—Water conservation.   4. Drought-tolerant
plants—United States. 5. Native plants for cultivation—United States. I. Title. II.
Title: Water-conserving gardens & landscapes.   III. Series.
SB475.83.043   1992
635.9'5—dc20   91-51124
                                                                                                            CIP

INTRODUCTION

Midway between Los Angeles and Carmel on the California coast lies Santa Barbara, a town that has long prided itself on the magnificence of its private and public gardens. It is an affluent town, home to ex-presidents and movie stars, and the beauty of its gardens is a major tourist attraction.

In February, 1991, however, dead trees lined the road into Santa Barbara. Gardens and parks were withered and brown as though a tremendous blight had hit the town. The unthinkable had happened. The authorities had shut off water to all landscaping within the city limits as California water reservoirs dried up in the fifth year of drought.

In the following month, a series of storms moved into California that were accompanied by heavy rain and snowfall in the Sierras, and the ban on landscape water was temporarily suspended. It will be years, however, before Santa Barbara's gardens and lawns recover; the water shortage crisis in California is far from over.

The drought and water cutoff in Santa Barbara and other communities did have a positive aspect: It focused attention on the growing problem of fresh water shortages in the West and created a tremendous public and legislative interest in xeriscape landscaping. This interest is now spreading beyond the West as other states face their own dwindling fresh water supplies. Water rationing and fines for excessive water use are fast becoming a fact of life in most of the West as state and local governments enact water conservation legislation.

As part of this water conservation effort, there is a growing trend to include provisions in both local and state legislation that specify the use of drought-resistant or water-conserving landscaping.

It is quite possible that similar legislation may appear in other localities nationwide in the coming years because the shortage of

Xeriscaping is a new gardening and landscaping approach that is gaining popularity as it becomes obvious that fresh water sources are becoming more scarce and expensive. According to Professor Henry W. Art in *The Wildflower Gardener's Guide: California, Desert Southwest, and Northern Mexico Edition* (Garden Way Publishing, 1990),

The term "xeriscaping" is derived from the Greek word xeros *meaning "dry" and is applied to techniques that reduce the water required to maintain gardens....Xeriscaping stresses the establishment of landscapes adapted to the arid environments around them, rather than trying to transplant and maintain water-consumptive landscapes from the humid East or tropics. Included among the several techniques used to create water-thrifty gardens and landscapes are: reducing the areas devoted to lawns, planting water-conserving plants, using the water-holding capacity of soils, grouping plants with similar water requirements close together and, if needed, installing microirrigation systems that most efficiently meet the plants' water needs.*

(See the Source List on page 146 for the address of the National Xeriscape Council).

fresh water (more correctly termed potable water, which means fit to drink) is not confined to the West. For example, even with 40 to 65 inches of rainfall annually, southern Florida is short of fresh water. Residents of Cape Coral and other Gulf Coast cities were fined heavily for watering their dry lawns during the drought of 1988 and 1989.

Even without periodic droughts, many other parts of the nation are facing a critical, long-term shortage of fresh water that is due to the widespread contamination of rivers, lakes, and groundwater reservoirs with pesticides, nitrates, and toxic chemical residues.

You need not fear, though, that by adopting water-conserving and drought-resistant gardening you must forgo your jade green turf and rose garden for a dusty, lackluster patch. On the contrary, xeriscape gardens can be as colorful and as vibrant and pleasing to the eye as any pampered, water-hungry, backyard retreat.

It is natural for gardeners to assume a larger interest and role in conservation and environmental protection. The water-conserving garden is an important expression of that concern. The goal of the water-conserving garden is very simple: to create a landscape environment that not only

Water-Conserving Gardens and Landscapes

looks beautiful, but that needs the least amount of water to stay beautiful. Home owners have found that such gardens not only trim their water bills and reduce maintenance time, but also increase the value of their property and improve environmental conditions.

The growing popularity of low-water-use gardening also reflects a changing lifestyle in which all the adults in the majority of households work outside the home. A carefree, low-maintenance garden likewise appeals to the occasional weekend or monthly gardener who wants a good looking garden, but does not have the daily hours that are needed to keep a garden "picture perfect." Not surprisingly, the lower maintenance aspect has also attracted the attention of commercial property owners. Water-conserving land-scaping not only saves on water costs, but also does not require a small army of landscape workers to keep it looking good.

My own interest in xeriscape gardening began after four years of struggling to turn the five acres of very dry, very sandy property that surrounded my former miniranch home in the Mojave Desert into a green oasis. I became intimately acquainted with the problems of living in a desert: hardpan, alkaline soils, the calcification of hard well water, blocked irrigation lines, the sandblasting quality of desert wind storms, and the persistence and appetites of desert animals — birds, field mice, jackrabbits, and gophers. I made every possible mistake.

I finally did discover that working with nature is far more rewarding and less complicated than trying to work against it. If I had known when I began what I now know about water-conserving gardening, I would have had my oasis with far less work and would have reduced my considerable water bill by two-thirds.

Putting in a water-conserving garden may seem like a small step toward ecological sanity, but it is a start. In addition to the tangible rewards of a lower water bill, the ability to survive drought condi-tions, and the reduction of garden maintenance, there are the intangible rewards of being more in tune with nature and of doing something to conserve earth's most vital and precious resource — fresh water.

This book is designed to introduce you to a gardening approach that is not only materially rewarding, but also makes you feel like a friend of Mother Nature, rather than an adversary.

IT ALL BEGINS WITH A PLAN

Not only would you not dream of building a house without a plan, but neither should you build a house without a landscape. Well-planned and well-maintained landscaping enhances your home by increasing the enjoyment of those who occupy it and by adding considerably to its value.

A successful, eye-pleasing, and practical water-conserving garden requires careful planning in the initial stages. This is not to say that there is a rigid formula that must be followed. As in any field, however, an understanding of the basics is necessary before one can successfully introduce innovation. The design tips that are given here represent the experience of gardeners and horticulturists over many years and whose efforts have culminated in today's low-water-use garden. In water-conserving gardens, for instance, plants and trees are zoned into areas of similar water use. A garden that is laid out with the following design basics will benefit by greatly reduced maintenance and water use in later years.

The plants and trees in our gardens originate from all over the world — from steaming Amazonian jungles to the arid Australian outback, from Russia's frozen tundra to the hot savannahs of Africa, to every region of the North American continent. Plants have been bred and crossbred to strengthen certain characteristics or to hasten their adaptation to other regions, but there are limits as to how far this adaptation can be pushed. For example, a Mediterranean-type vine, such as cup-of-gold *(Solandra maxima),* can do quite well in western gardens where frost is a rare visitor, but it is unable to survive a midwestern or eastern winter.

The most successful gardeners are those who have become environmentally smart. All it takes is a little time to understand the effects of their particular climate on plants and to concentrate on those plants that have adapted to that climate or have been bred especially for those climatic conditions. The interest in gardening with native species has occurred not only because more people are responding to the need to preserve these valuable species, but also because so many of the native varieties are spectacularly beautiful when they are given the care and attention of a garden setting; equally important, native species are extremely hardy.

Fortunately, very detailed climate maps are available from nurseries, seed catalogue companies, local horticultural societies, and university and college cooperative extension offices (usually listed under "County" in the white pages of your telephone book). Seeds, plants, and rootstock are usually tagged with the climate zone in which they will succeed. Personnel at your local nursery also can help you choose the appropriate plants for your locale.

The xeriscape gardener will want to look beyond the obvious climate conditions in their region to take advantage of microclimates. These are very localized areas where the slope of the land, the effect of a nearby hill or canyon, or the influence of a lake or the ocean create variations from the climate norm. For instance, experienced gardeners know that colder air sinks downhill and that the low corner of a garden or hollow will be colder than its surroundings. Areas on higher ground, especially if they face south or southwest, as well as areas that receive reflected sunlight from south- and west-facing structures, generally will be warmer than surrounding sites.

Water-Conserving Gardens and Landscapes

Although this warmth can be an advantage, you also must consider that these same areas will experience a far higher water evaporation rate.

Some very clever things can be done if you understand the microclimates in your garden. For example, you could strategically place shade trees or ground covers to reduce both the temperature and water loss during the summer, yet allow the sun to enter the same area in the winter.

If you recently have moved into an area, get as much information about your new locale from neighbors and local nurseries as possible; then assess those facts as they relate to your own observations. Frankly, not all of the advice will be accurate or beneficial. For example, one very experienced gardener in my region told me, "You can't grow tomatoes in the desert past the month of June." I, nevertheless, set out juicy beefsteak tomatoes and two varieties of miniature tomatoes and collected tomatoes all summer long and well into the fall.

You may wish to invest a little money (as little as $100 and sometimes less) to have a professional landscape designer or architect evaluate your site. For a small garden or part of a garden, a professional will draw a site plan for between $200 and $500. Compared to what you will be spending on plants, water, mulch, fertilizer, plus your time over the coming years, it is not a lot of money to make sure that you are starting off on the right foot. If you want a professional to draw up a complete landscaping plan, it will cost from $500 to $1000 for an average home. To draw up a plan and supervise the installation, professionals charge either a percentage of the total cost, a set fee, or an hourly rate.

My assumption in writing this book, though, is that the reader is going to plan and plant his or her own water-conserving garden. After all, that is where most of the fun and creativity lies.

THE BASE PLAN

First, draw up a preliminary plan that is based on the type of site that you have and your own and your family's requirements and desires.

To assess your site, look at soil conditions, drainage, slopes, the direction of the prevailing wind, and where the sun falls in the

morning, afternoon, and evening. Evaluate existing qualities —
what rocks, slopes, trees, or plants do you want to retain and make a
part of the new design?

Take a decorator's viewpoint with your garden. What is the
overall feeling that you want to convey: a formal landscape with
sharply defined edges and geometrically shaped areas, a natural look
with its open spaces and rough textures, or a rustic appearance with
naturally shaped plants that droop and fold over weathered boards
and railroad ties?

Whether tropical or woodsy, formal or informal, or a mixture of
all of these, the next key question is what is your greatest interest? Is
it function or beauty? Do you want the garden and other areas around
the house to be a beautiful setting? Do you want your landscape
divided into function areas: an area where children will play, a patio
for barbecues and relaxation, a space for a hot tub, gazebo, or
vegetable garden?

When you design outdoor areas with specific functions in mind,
consider the effect of the early morning light, the hot afternoon
sunshine, and the cool of evening. Primarily, a garden should serve
the interests of the gardener and his or her family and also be
attractive. A garden that successfully meets these two requirements
is going to be a winner.

Look to the future. If you have children now, their needs will
change as they grow. A sandbox and play area can be planned so that
it is easily converted to a vegetable garden later. When you consider
where you want children to play, be sure that the area will be visible
from the house.

With regard to local zoning laws, decide how much privacy you
will need from your neighbor and how best to preserve the most
scenic views. Also consider special needs, such as a greenhouse or
garden work area where you can grow seedlings and store tools,
fertilizer, and compost. If you want to have a large deck or patio area,
but cannot afford the entire project right now, build the deck or patio
in sections.

Next, decide what you are prepared to spend. What is the budget
for this project? Can you do it quickly for an immediate effect, or will
you spread it out and do the project in phases?

With these decisions in mind, on a large sheet of graph paper,
draw a plan to scale that shows property boundary lines, house,

fences, existing trees, shrubs, walkways, irrigation lines, and locations of outside water outlets. Obviously, this is the logical way to proceed, but when it comes to garden design, logic is not everything.

Personally, I prefer the create-as-you-go method of designing, which relies heavily on intuition. If it works, that is wonderful. If it does not, try something else. I like to walk around with a stick and draw the outline of paths, borders, and irrigation lines on the ground;

The Base Plan

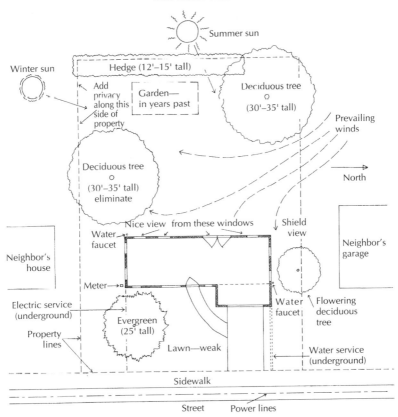

you also could use tape or a ball of twine. You should not feel constricted when designing your garden or landscape and particularly not when planning water-conserving gardens. Experiment, have fun, do it your way.

If you cannot or do not want to lay out an entire garden, do it in small stages. For example, you could have a three-year plan. After analyzing your existing landscape with the purpose of reducing water usage, decide on the final plants and hardscapes that you envision on your property in three years. Then in the first year, install all hardscapes, renovate or create your irrigation system, add one or two shade trees and some ground covers, and reduce the lawn area. The second year, add shrubs, more shade trees and ground covers, and further reduce the lawn. The third year, adjust your irrigation system for the final number of plants, and add more shrubs, trees, or ground covers until you accomplish your final landscaping goal.

Water-conserving landscape design and gardening is a wide open field right now. Do not be intimidated by advice and do not be afraid to make mistakes. By following the advice in this book, you will reduce mistakes considerably.

ZONING THE LANDSCAPE

A key element in designing a water-conserving garden is to group plants into three or four microclimate zones according to their mutual requirements for water, sunshine, and soil pH (measure of soil acidity or alkaline condition). If you mix drought-resistant plants with those that require more water, for instance, you will end up "drowning" the drought-resistant plants.

As with any other plants, good soil preparation, heavy mulching to reduce evaporation from the soil, and regulated, low-pressure, drip-style irrigation will greatly reduce water needs — sometimes by as much as 70 percent.

Decks, patios, paving stones, gravel, or mulched areas can act as transition zones among high-water-use plants that are close to the house, moderate- to low-water-use plants, and no-water-use areas. The idea is to blend these areas together so they flow naturally into the other in a manner that is both pleasing to the eye and practical. Gray, gray-blue, or silvery shrubs are ideal for transitional plantings among different garden zones. By restricting the transitional plantings to one species or similar species, the design of the whole garden is tied together and provides continuity.

High-water-use zone. It makes sense to group your favorite high-water-use plants, no matter how water demanding, in a small, oasislike area close to the house. These are the plants that you want to see everyday. By placing them close to the house, they will be easier

10

to water and less likely to be overlooked. Raised beds or containers are ideal for these plants because you can closely control soil quality and watering.

The idea that every home must have a lawn as the focal point of its landscaping stems more from transplanted notions of Victorian designers than from practicality or common sense. In this country, the amount of time and money spent fighting weeds and crabgrass, spraying insecticides, mowing, raking, fertilizing, and watering the average lawn can be astronomical. Drought-resistant ground covers and other water-conserving alternatives not only do away with all this expenditure of time and money, but also can improve the appearance of the property with their forms, textures, and colors.

If you must have a lawn, realize that it requires the most water of any garden area. More than half of the water consumed by a typical single-family residence is used to irrigate the lawn. At the very least, think seriously about reducing the size of the lawn by replacing sections of it with areas of hardscape or drought-resistant ground covers, shrubs, and trees. Think about creating a lawn that is an oasis or strip of green — an accent, rather than a large expanse of water-demanding grass.

Moderate-water-use zone. This would include areas with ground covers, annuals, and vegetable gardens. These areas are best watered on a timer with drip irrigation or manually as needed with drip or soaker hoses (see Chapter Six). As a general rule, stay away from conventional sprinklers, which result in high water losses due to wind, evaporation, overwatering, and runoff.

Low-water-use zone. Plants, trees, and ground covers within this zone should be on a low-volume drip-irrigation system (see Chapter Six). The plants and trees may be drought resistant, but may require more water than is available from natural precipitation.

No-water-use zone. This area includes hardscapes (patios, decks, walkways) and established drought-resistant plants and trees that can survive on natural precipitation only. Even drought-resistant plants do require watering when first planted in order to develop the deep root systems that will sustain them in later years. Planting in the fall is urged because the ground is cooler, and there is more natural moisture available. Fall planting gives the new plant a full winter of root growth and adaptation before facing the summer heat.

11

It All Begins With a Plan

First Season Care is Critical

There are two major mistakes that you can make with drought-resistant plants. The first is to set them in the ground from the container or as a bare-root plant and expect them to make it on their own. The second is to overwater them once they have become established. Overwatering is particularly deadly for these plants because many of them are semidormant during the heat of summer. If you water them at this time, the roots are susceptible to root rot and other bacterial infections that thrive in warm, wet soil.

For a plant to become drought tolerant, it must extend its roots far enough to contact the moisture that is held deep in the soil from winter snow and rain. It is this moisture that carries the plant through the summer. In order for the plant to do this, you must water the soil slowly and very deeply at the time of planting in the fall. If winter rains in your area are scarce, you will have to water the plant each time that the soil dries out at the depth of the root ball. You also will need to water deeply and thoroughly during the plant's first summer at least once a month, and perhaps more often, depending upon the climate and the plant. By the time the second summer rolls around, most of the plants will no longer need summer water, or at the most they only will need an occasional deep soaking. The time to water is at night or in the early morning when the soil is cooler.

PUTTING IT ALL TOGETHER

With your base plan of the property showing all existing structures, trees, and boundaries, trace the fixed features (house, driveway, property boundaries, and established trees) that will remain. Start sketching in the additional features that you want your landscape to have eventually. Paper is cheap, so at this stage you can be as fanciful and expansive as you like.

This is also a good time to decide on irrigation systems and where the lines will run. With a little forethought, you can avoid the chore of having to route water lines around a patio, deck, or walkway (see Chapter Six, page 71).

In my opinion, drip irrigation is the preferred way to irrigate the water-conserving garden or any other garden. I have heard people say, "Why should I spend money on drip irrigation when I can get the same results with soaker hoses or bubblers?" Well, consider water savings as high as 70 percent over conventional irrigation methods. Consider fewer weeds, stronger plants, and an increased vegetable and fruit yield. Drip irrigation is the most efficient irrigation system available. Try it, and I know you will be convinced of its merits. (See Chapter Six for a complete discussion of drip irrigation systems.)

LANDSCAPE DESIGN TIPS

The most obvious plants and trees to choose when you are planning a xeriscape garden are those that are naturally drought resistant, either native or imported. Many drought-enduring ever-green trees and shrubs from the Southwest will also flourish as far east as Philadelphia. Cacti and many of the so-called "luscious" varieties of drought-resistant plants that grace many western gardens with their subtle shades of gray, green, and purple foliage and spectacular floral bloom, however, are strictly for very mild winter zones. Although they can be grown in colder regions in containers, they must be taken inside to a heated environment during the winter.

Advice on the selection of low-water-use plants can be found in Chapter Seven. In this early planning stage, however, be sure to think of a plant's ultimate size. You do not want endlessly to prune and trim back a plant that you thought was going to be a small patch of color, but at maturity might take over your entire garden.

Trees and shrubs should be planted first since they take much longer to develop than other plantings. Take the time to make the right choices. Consider what you want that tree or shrub to do for you? How do you want it to look? What will its function be? Will it serve for shade, privacy, or simply be ornamental? Check your design against the actual site. Where does the sun fall in the morning, afternoon, and evening? Remember that the angle of the sun changes with the seasons. The summer sun is high in the sky; in the winter, it is lower so its rays come at a lower angle.

One of the priorities of landscape design is to moderate the effect of the sun. A shaded roof can keep a house 10 to 20 degrees cooler than an unshaded roof. (If you are thinking of installing solar power

It All Begins With a Plan

in the future, the solar panels need full sunlight to operate efficiently. The most common site for the solar panels is the roof, but where there is room, siting the panels on the ground near the house can be as effective and much simpler to install and maintain.)

Particularly in desert regions, you will want to have as much shade from the sun as possible in the summer, yet allow the sun to warm the house in the winter. For this reason, plant sturdy deciduous shade trees that lose their leaves in the winter and allow the sun to warm and brighten the house. An energy-saving design could feature an evergreen in such a way that its high canopy gives shade from the more direct summer sun, but in the winter allows the lower-angled sun's rays to warm the house.

Wind, especially in midwestern states and desert areas, is another natural force to consider. It picks up dust, dirt, and sand that find their way into your house no matter how tightly you close it up. Wind can whip up a dust cloud that suddenly smacks you in the face just when you are enjoying a meal on your patio. Cold winter winds that drive against unprotected windows and the sides of your house also can increase your fuel bill. A windbreak of trees, shrubs, or a foliage screen can offer protection and help to lower the fuel bill.

For year-round windbreaks, it is difficult to top evergreens. Choose an evergreen or conifer with broadleaf foliage that reaches to the ground, such as cypress *(Cupressus* spp.), juniper *(Juniperus* spp.), and certain pines *(Pinus* spp.). Such a screen will reduce the force of the wind and filter out sand, dirt, and dust. It also will keep the wind from blowing away your precious and expensive topsoil.

You can check prevailing winds by tying a ribbon or strips of cloth to fence posts or to a stake that is high enough to catch the main wind and not just eddies. If you are new to the area, ask your neighbors if the wind changes direction in the summer and winter. In high wind areas, just look at which direction the trees are leaning to find the prevailing wind.

The priorities in planting natural windbreaks or erecting artificial barriers are the following:

1. Take into account the direction of the prevailing winds. You want the windscreen to stand approximately at right angles to the prevailing wind.

2. The general rule is that you place a windbreak at a distance that is three to seven times its height upwind of the area that it protects. A row of trees that is 20 feet high, for instance, will protect an area 60 to 140 feet away.

3. A natural windbreak has the advantage of being porous; it allows some wind to flow through. This slows the wind considerably over a much greater distance than if you had a solid windscreen. A solid windscreen, such as a wall, blocks the wind completely, but creates a pocket of still air that extends for only a short distance; then the wind that has been diverted upward comes down with even greater force. A solid windbreak only should be used when it is placed very close to the house.

The location of trees around the house is important because it can affect the ventilation in your home. The overall aim is to reduce the destructive effects of prevailing winds without losing the cooling effect of summer breezes. Since every house and garden is different, depending on location, elevation, the nearness of other buildings and trees, it is difficult to be more explicit. What I can suggest is that before you erect a permanent structure, such as a wall or hedge, put up a temporary screen or a latticework that is covered with canvas, shade cloth, or a fast growing annual vine, and see if it creates the effect that you want.

Hot south and west walls in the summer also can be kept cool with any of numerous and beautiful vines, such as some *Clematis* species — sweet autumn clematis *(C. paniculata)* or the big petal clematis *(C. macropetala),* which is a favorite in northern states for its hardiness and azure blue flowers. If the wall is going to require periodic painting, it is advisable to erect a trellis or wood or metal frame that is hinged at the bottom and secured to the wall with cleats and bolts. Trellises that are covered with a deciduous grapevine can provide excellent and eye-pleasing shade. Grapes are fast growers and also produce excellent fruit, yet they drop their foliage to allow the winter sun to warm the house. Other fast but temporary covers include annuals, such as morning-glory *(Ipomoea* spp.*)* or perennials, such as queen's-wreath *(Antigonon leptopus).* (See Chapter Seven for more plant suggestions and descriptions.)

15

Finally, take into account the effect of glare and reflected heat from paved areas and even bare soil or gravel. This reflected heat will increase the temperature of the air and nearby buildings. It can be moderated or eliminated by planting shade trees or drought- and heat-resistant ground covers, such as rosemary *(Rosmarinus* spp.) or dwarf junipers *(Juniperus* spp.). Rocky or paved areas have a particular advantage in the winter; they store up the sun's heat and release it at night. That released heat is perfect for cold sensitive plants that would otherwise suffer in unprotected areas of the garden.

If you are bothered by the barren look of your landscape before it properly "grows in," you can get an instant effect by putting in fast growing, temporary plants alongside the permanent plants. Annuals, such as cucumber-leaf sunflower *(Helianthus debilis),* balsam *(Impatiens balsamina),* or fountain grass *(Pennisetum setaceum),* make excellent, temporary hedges. Herbaceous perennials that tend to die out after a few years, such as Colorado columbine *(Aquilegia caerulea),* can be planted and will have died out by the time the more permanent plants fill out. Alternatively, use containers of fast growing plants to liven up the area until the permanent citizens of the garden take over.

When you finally have a plan that you are happy with, take the time to walk around your property with it and mentally picture how it will look when it is planted — where the shade will be, what the color effects will be when plants are in bloom, and how the irrigation system will operate. Now is the time to make changes until it all feels "just right." Then execute your design, but do not be too rigid about it. There are bound to be mistakes and changes; it happens even with the most carefully planned gardens. As you plant, the garden will become more real, and other, perhaps better, ideas will occur.

ADVICE FROM A GARDEN DESIGN EXPERT

Because of the limited usefulness of plans and photographs of other people's gardens since home owners differ in their likes, dislikes, needs, and desires, and since each site is totally different and requires different design considerations, I thought it useful to get the viewpoint of an expert garden and landscape design architect with extensive experience in low-water-use plants and garden design.

Shirley A. Kerins, ASLA, is a certified landscape architect in Pasadena, California, with degrees in ornamental horticulture and landscape architecture from the University of Rhode Island. For the past 12 years, she has been a horticultural consultant to the famed Huntington Botanical Gardens in Pasadena where she serves as the manager of plant production and plant sales and is the curator of the Herb Garden. She designed the Kallan Memorial Perennial Garden at the Los Angeles State and County Arboretum and the New Zealand Garden for the Huntington Botanical Gardens, as well as a wide variety of conventional and water-conserving gardens for home owners with homes that range from tract homes to large suburban estates. She is also a vice president and member of the board of directors of the Southern California Horticultural Society, past president of the Orange County Horticultural Society, and founder of the Orange County Herb Society.

One of the first things that you have to ask yourself explains Kerins, regardless if the garden is to be drought tolerant, is what do you want the garden to do for you? Do you want to use it for outdoor dining, for a collection of plants, or for a beautiful view?

Once you establish the purposes of your garden, look at the various different areas and address each area separately. If it is an area that is going to have a lot of furniture or a lot of hardscape, then decide on the type of hardscape — porous paving, granite, gravel, stepping stones, or paving with nonmortared joints.

If the area is going to be plant-oriented, there are four aspects to consider: the condition of the soil, the choice of plant material, the arrangement and spacing of plants with similar water needs, and the importance of mulching.

Starting first with the soil, incorporate organic amendments into the soil so that it drains well, yet retains moisture for the plants. Organic amendments basically give the soil both large and small pore spaces. These pore spaces are necessary so that the plants can breathe and the soil retains sufficient moisture reserves to keep it from drying out between waterings. There is nothing magical about the amendment that goes into the ground; kitchen waste and garden trimmings that are turned into compost are the best amendment. The key is to condition the soil so that it is as perfect as possible in the growing area.

It All Begins With a Plan

Choice of plant material comes next, along with their arrangement in the garden. In addition to your usual favorites, you must consider the size of the plants at maturity, their requirements for sunlight, and their water use. Then group plants with similar water needs together. Grouping plants with similar water needs is one of the easiest things that the home owner can do to ensure a beautiful garden that also saves water. Once the soil has been conditioned properly, it is easy to grow almost any plant you wish. For example, if you want to grow roses, do not locate them near plants with lower water needs.

The spacing of plants also is important. A garden that is designed from scratch usually takes five years to reach its full effect. In high-sunshine temperate areas that time can be as short as three years. Check the mature size of the plants and space the plants accordingly. If the plants are placed too close together, you will be endlessly pruning or relocating plants to avoid overcrowding as they reach maturity.

Mulching is another consideration. Whenever possible, Shirley Kerins favors the use of low ground cover plants that are used as mulch and set out in varying layers. The mulch plants keep the soil cool and reduce surface evaporation, while they provide the garden with a lush, green look. Mulch plants do not blow away as shredded bark and other light mulches do, and when you want to make changes in your garden, the mulch plants can be dug into the soil where they will condition the soil and help nourish other plants.

Kerins spends a lot of time convincing people that a drought-resistant or water-conserving garden does not mean austerity or deprivation. She points out that home owners can have most of what they want if they follow the rules about soil conditioning and grouping plants by water needs.

In gardening, knowledge equals success. To be successful in any type of gardening, but especially in water-conserving gardening, an understanding of how and why plants grow, of the nature of the soil, and of the role of water and nutrients is essential. In the following chapters, we will cover the basics of plant growth and of the soil, nutrients, and water that are essential to their survival with particular attention to drought-resistant or low-water-use species.

Water-Conserving Gardens and Landscapes

GARDEN HARDSCAPES — MATERIALS AND CONSTRUCTION

The use of hardscapes (patios, terraces, or paths) in gardens is nothing new. The ancient Greeks built their houses around open central courtyards. The interior courtyard design was primarily for security purposes and only secondarily for privacy. The Greeks, however, planted trees and hung baskets of fragrant flowers and herbs in honor of various gods and goddesses in their courtyards.

Eventually, many of the Mediterranean countries adopted this practice, especially the Italians and the Spanish. This inner courtyard and garden patio concept arrived here with the conquistadors. Some of the finest, Spanish-style patio courtyard gardens can still be seen in some of the old missions in the Southwest, in the Old Quarter of New Orleans, and in parts of Florida. In the Southwest, it is still a very popular concept that either follows the original design of an inner courtyard garden or has been adapted to a conventional backyard.

One of the key elements in xeriscape garden design is the integration of plants with hardscapes and the extensive use of gravel, stone, pebbles, or organic mulches to define and set off different garden zones. The emphasis on hardscapes of brick, stone, and vine covered arbors also has found a natural extension in this new garden concept. Hardscapes require no watering and very little maintenance, while providing practical user-oriented spaces. When thoughtfully incorporated into the overall garden design, they tie the garden together into a unified house and garden landscape of charm and practicality. A landscape designer may describe it as tonal contrasts or the contrast between the inert and the organic. Nevertheless, the combination of drought-resistant plants and hardscapes creates a soothing and pleasing effect that defies accurate description. The closest description would be the word "harmony."

Perhaps the foremost practitioners of design harmony today are the Japanese, whose hardscapes of patterned sand and gravel are the backdrop to a select choice of rocks and plants. With this discriminating simplicity, they create gardens of contemplation that border on sculpture. Although most of us can admire such aesthetics, we do not necessarily want it for our backyard. The Japanese influence, however, certainly can be seen in modern landscape design, especially in many of the new water-conserving garden and landscape designs.

The xeriscape garden is a garden in the true sense — a place to make contact with nature, a place to relax, a place to grow things, and a place to create an individual statement in color, form, and texture that is both a personal pleasure to behold and a pleasure for others to observe. It can be as spare and aesthetic as a Japanese garden or as lush and woodsy as an English garden; it also can be almost anything in between.

Most importantly, the low-water-use or drought-resistant plants that are used in the water-conserving gardening approach do not have fragile natures. They are hardy, enduring, and have great survival potential. Let's now discover how to make sure that those hardscapes that you build also will be enduring.

The advantages of paved or gravel areas and wooden decks are fairly obvious: They require no watering or maintenance; they provide areas for relaxation and entertainment; they make great staging areas for containers, such as pots, tubs, or hanging baskets.

Retaining walls, pathways, and areas that can be hardscaped with gravel, crushed stone, pebbles, or bark mulches are best constructed **after** any underground irrigation lines have been installed and **before** actual planting begins.

20

Porous Versus Nonporous Construction of Hardscapes

Porous construction of hardscapes, such as the open place-ment of wooden decks, stepping stones, brick, flagstone, or broken concrete, allow rainwater to penetrate the soil and help to replenish irreplaceable groundwater supplies. Solid construction of hardscapes, such as concrete or mortared brick and mortared paving stone, can create washouts in the garden. Most often with these constructions, the rainwater is directed into drains or into the street where it is carried away by sewers and lost to the soil. There are very few communities, which include many in even high annual rainwater areas, where the groundwater levels have not dropped drastically over the years because of urban sprawl and the subsequent paving of what were once natural drainage areas.

If home owners began to insist on porous construction of hardscapes wherever possible, it would be a step toward the replenishment of vital groundwater supplies. As it is, rainwa-ter that is allowed to percolate into the soil through these hardscapes will at least replenish the moisture levels of your garden and cut down considerably on the water needs of your plants.

GARDEN PATHS

A garden path is more than a means of walking around the garden without trampling plants or getting your shoes dirty, it is an impor-tant design element of the garden. The path itself and the materials used for its construction help tie the landscape together. Stepping stones, gravel, wood, concrete rounds, cobblestones, or bricks have all been used in garden paths. The hardscaping material you choose depends on the garden itself — its size, shape, overall color, and character.

To me a path is a somewhat magical thing. I do not want it to look like a driveway or a straight line. The most pleasing of all paths are natural paths where people have walked for generations, where the path has skirted natural obstacles, or where it has merely followed the easiest lay of the land. When laying out paths in your garden, remember that a straight path will divide an area and make it seem smaller. A path that wanders with gentle curves will make the garden seem larger.

Natural path. The way to make an earthen path is simple. Soak the soil thoroughly; strip about 2 or 3 inches of soil from the top and remove all grass and weed roots. The path needs to be at least 3 feet wide, preferably 4 feet. Level the earth after weeding and tamp it firmly into place, either by walking on it or using an earth-tamping tool. Make the path slightly higher in the center, so water will run off toward the edges. If you have a roller, use it to tamp the soil because the more firmly the soil is packed the better the path. If the path gets out of shape from use, wet it down, and tamp the soil again.

Gravel path. The gravel path can be prepared in the same way as the natural path by laying the gravel directly on the soil. It will not withstand hard wear, however, and in wet weather will become soft and springy. To make a much more permanent and resilient path, excavate the soil to about 7 inches below grade and lay down a 5-inch layer of crushed stone ($1/2$ to $1 1/2$ inch size) or coarse decomposed granite for a foundation. Either tamp down the stone or granite or use a roller to compact it. Cover the path with a layer of black polyethylene sheeting to prevent weed growth. Puncture the plastic with a fork so water can drain away. Spread a layer of $1/2$-inch natural river washed gravel over the plastic, water it down, and tamp or roll it well. (Gravel that is smaller than $1/2$ inch will get kicked away; gravel that is larger than $1/2$ inch will be difficult to walk on.) Add another layer of gravel and repeat the procedure until you have the final thickness.

To make an even tidier path that will not get ragged at the edges, dig a small trench on either side of the path and install a 2x4 board on its edge or use bricks to border the path and keep it contained.

You can also add flat stepping stones to a gravel path. Omit the header boards or bricks to give the path a more natural, meandering look that is similar to the stepping stones' approach. The gravel and stones can blend into ground cover on either side of the path.

Bark path. For a nice looking springy path, you can use fir bark, which is inexpensive and easy to lay down. Use a $1/2$-inch or 1-inch diameter bark for paths. Smaller pieces will blow or wash away. You

Water-Conserving Gardens and Landscapes

will need a minimum of 2 inches of bark, preferably 3 inches. Fir bark, however, deteriorates fairly rapidly, and the material may have to be replaced annually.

For a more permanent bark path, use tanbark, which is the bark that is used for tanning leather. Tanbark dries almost immediately after wetting, never gets muddy even during the heaviest rains, and lasts for many years. A 3-inch layer makes a very durable, pleasingly springy, reddish brown path that is quite durable. After spreading the tanbark, soak it well and roll it. Tanbark is not easy to find these days and is usually sold only in areas where tanneries are located. If your local nursery cannot help, and there is a tannery in your area, call and ask them if they have bark for sale. Licorice root is said to be a good substitute, and it is almost as durable as tanbark. Check with your local nursery.

Brick path. Brick paths have great charm as they mellow with age. The only drawback is the cost. That cost rises if you happen to be in a region where frost penetrates and stays in the ground for any length of time; a brick or flagstone path will require a thick crushed stone or gravel foundation or a combination of coarse builder's sand and gravel foundation to prevent frost heaves in the path. In regions where frost does not linger and penetrate the ground, bricks can be laid directly on a cushion of coarse builder's sand.

Estimating Gravel

1. Multiply the length of the area to be covered by its width.
2. Multiply this resulting figure by the decimal number below which corresponds to your desired depth of gravel.

Depth in Inches	Decimal Number
1	.083
2	.17
3	.25
4	.33
5	.42
6	.50
7	.58
8	.67
9	.75
10	.84
11	.92
12	1.00

3. To express the product in cubic yards, the measure in which gravel is usually sold, divide the last resulting figure by 27.

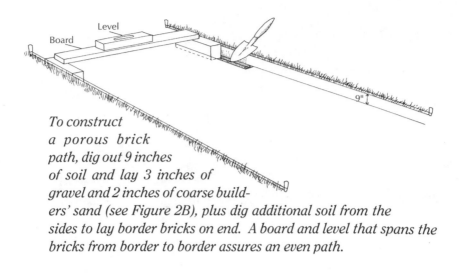

To construct
a porous brick
path, dig out 9 inches
of soil and lay 3 inches of
gravel and 2 inches of coarse build-
ers' sand (see Figure 2B), plus dig additional soil from the
sides to lay border bricks on end. A board and level that spans the
bricks from border to border assures an even path.

VIEW FROM ABOVE

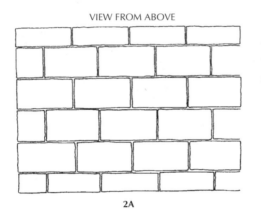

2A

*Bricks can be laid in many
different patterns; the stag-
gered pattern shown here
is easy to build.*

CROSS SECTION

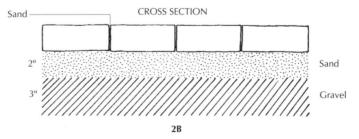

2B

*Assure adequate drainage by layering gravel,
then sand over the soil before laying the bricks.*

Water-Conserving Gardens and Landscapes

When a brick path is laid in sand without mortaring, the edges of the path need a rigid border to keep the bricks from wandering. Without a restraining border or head board, unmortared bricks tend to creep apart as you walk on them.

If you must have a mortared brick or paving stone path, you will need a concrete base to prevent the bricks from moving and destroying the mortar bond.

In northern regions where heavy ground frost is routine in the winter, the path will have to be excavated to 12 inches below the grade, and a 6-inch layer of gravel will have to be put down. First, lay down 3 inches of gravel, water it down, and tamp or roll it. Then lay the second 3-inch layer and repeat. A 3-inch layer of base concrete is then laid over the gravel (1 part cement, 3 parts sand, 5 parts gravel).

Let the concrete set for 24 hours. Lay the bricks in the desired pattern on a thin smear of mortar (1 part cement, 3 parts sand). Wait until the cement has set hard and the bricks are firmly in place before filling the joints. Narrow joints of ¼ inch or less can be filled with a dry mixture of sand and cement (1 part cement, 2 parts sand). Sweep the mixture into the joints; then sweep the bricks clean of the sand-cement mixture. Water the walk with a gentle spray until all the cement in the joints is thoroughly wet. If the joints between the bricks are large, use a wet jointing mixture (1 part cement, 2 parts sand). Pour it between the bricks and smooth and finish with a trowel.

A porous brick path without mortar that is laid on sand in a cold climate needs a similar foundation of gravel. After following the initial procedure of excavating below grade and laying down the gravel, spread a 2-inch layer of fine sand over the gravel and tamp or roll it firmly into place. Next, set the bricks in place and fill the joints with sand. Use a board on edge that is laid across the path to tamp the bricks down into an even surface.

Concrete path. Broken concrete or a combination of concrete, brick, cobbles, pebbles, or stepping stones can be used to make paths that are both durable and attractive. Broken concrete is cheap and makes sound ecological sense; it is usually buried in a landfill by contractors after they tear down an old building or replace a sidewalk. If you ask them, many contractors will let you take the concrete away without charge.

The broken pieces of concrete are laid in a bed of sand in a patchwork pattern by fitting the broken pieces to make a random paving effect. The spaces between the chunks of concrete can be filled with sand or planted with a low ground cover or grass. One manufacturer (Concrete Paver Systems of Los Angeles) is marketing Turf Stone, which are concrete blocks that are full of holes in which to grow grass or plants (see Source List on page 146 for address).

If you want a laid concrete path or driveway, you can also create the same effect by using wood frames to separate the path or driveway area into paving stone-size areas. The frames are made from 2x6 treated lumber. The frames serve as forms for the concrete, but remain in place as part of the pattern. Hammer a long nail into the adjoining pieces of wood at each corner. The nails will lock the concrete to the wood. Textured surfaces are made just before the concrete sets thoroughly. These can be made by swirling patterns with a wire brush or by pounding pebbles into the unset concrete. After the concrete has thoroughly set, the pebbles are washed and scrubbed.

There are also many types of interlocking paving stones on the market that are relatively easy to set by the home owner. Their drawback is that they are not porous. These paving stones come in brick sizes and are made from compressed concrete with a nonmatte finish. They are frequently used for decking around a swimming pool. They can be laid on a 2-inch sand bed. If frost is a problem, you will need a gravel and sand substructure (see instructions on page 25).

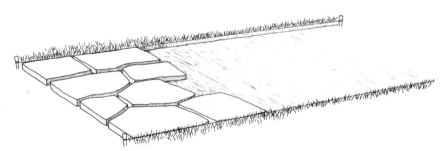

26

To build a flagstone path, outline the path with string, remove sod, and lay the flagstones on a layer of course builders' sand and a layer of gravel (see Figure 2B on page 24).

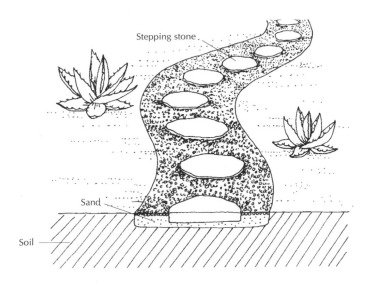

Stepping stone

Sand

Soil

Flagstone path. Flagstones make great garden paths. If you live near a stone-producing quarry, they can be relatively inexpensive, too. The stones are cut square or rectangular for a symmetrical path or irregularly cut for a random pattern effect. Again, flagstones can be laid on a sand cushion or a cement foundation with mortared joints (see "Brick path" on page 25). If the joints are filled with soil, the path will be porous and you will be able to grow various mosses or low, creeping rock plants between the stones; this considerably adds to the stones' charm and beauty.

Flagstones with either flat or irregular bottoms must be carefully laid so that all sections of the stone are touching the bed so that you do not wobble or teeter when you stand on them.

Stepping stone path. Done well, stepping stone paths are probably the most attractive garden path. Stepping stones come in such a wide variety of sizes and types that the option of style is almost endless. They also are easy to work with and allow rainwater to percolate into the soil.

Stepping stone paths are made to wander around trees and large rocks and in and out of shrubs. The only rule about laying down a stepping stone path is to use stones of a comfortable size, at least 3 inches thick and 12 to 15 inches wide, and to place them at even intervals and far enough apart to accommodate an easy stride from one stone to the next, which is about 18 inches.

27

Stepping stones can be natural rocks with a flat surface (sandstone or granite), chunks of granite slabs, commercially sold concrete rounds, sliced tree trunks, or a do-it-yourself combination of concrete and pebbles. Laying them is quite easy, but they should be set into the ground so that two-thirds of the stone is buried (see illustration on page 27). The stepping stone should stand a little above the level of the surrounding soil to prevent the soil from working its way over the stones. Do not dig until you have laid the stones on the ground in the position that you want them.

If you are using both small and large stones, place the large stones first, then work the smaller stones into the pattern. When you are ready to dig them in, mark the outline of the stone with the edge of a trowel before moving the stone. They then can be laid directly onto the subsoil or on a bed of 1 or 2 inches of coarse builder's sand.

SAND, GRAVEL, AND OTHER HARDSCAPES

Sand, gravel, pebbles, rocks, and other inorganic mulches allow water to percolate through to the soil and can be used in a variety of ways in the xeriscape garden: a ground cover beneath trees, a border, a setting for prize container plants, a divider among different zones of the garden, or a way to tie the garden design together and to unify the separate elements. Sand, gravel, or rocks can be used to great advantage in those problem areas where nothing seems to grow, in heavily shaded areas, or in difficult corners.

Sand can be purchased from most building supply yards in a variety of colors that range from stark white to umber, blue, and black. Do *not* use beach sand. It is too fine and will blow away in a strong wind or wash away in the rain. Sand makes a perfect stage-setting for distinctive, single shrubs, such as a clump of pampas grass *(Cortaderia selloana)*, New-Zealand-flax *(Phormium tenax)*, or for a single decorative tree, such as the wonderfully convoluted shore pine *(Pinus contorta)*.

Sand has been recommended by some gardeners as a mulch around shrubs; a 3- to 5-inch layer will keep the soil cool and help it to retain moisture. The only problem with using sand as a mulch is that if you want to change that area of the garden or need to condition the soil, you will have to dig the sand out of the way and then return it to the spot or replace it with new sand. That is the problem with all inorganic mulch materials. (Personally, I would rather use organic mulches or use ground cover plants as a living mulch. When these need replacing or you want to rearrange an area, organic mulches can be dug into the soil to condition it.)

To use sand as a hardscape, remove weeds and cover the area with black polyethylene sheeting that has been punctured with holes for drainage. Spread about 2 inches of sand and either tamp or roll it. Add a final 2-inch layer of sand and tamp or roll it in place. If you do not want anyone to walk on it, draw patterns in it with a fork or rake. If you want to place a few choice shrubs or decorative grasses in the sand, then plant these plants before laying down the polyethylene sheeting and the sand. Do not lay the plastic next to the plant stem; leave room for the plant to breathe and grow. With a few choice rocks or boulders, you can have your own miniature Japanese sand garden.

Gravel and crushed stone can also be used decoratively and as inorganic mulches. Like sand, they will not add anything to the soil, but they will keep it cool and help it to retain moisture. The best gravel to use for mulches is natural river washed gravel, which does not have the sharp edges of crushed stone. It is usually sold in sizes that range from $1/4$ inch to $2^1/4$ inches in diameter. You do not want to use gravel less than a $1/2$ inch in size because it gets kicked around, will end up where you do not want it, and rain will wash it away. You can use gravel in the same manner as sand by using black polyethylene sheeting to prevent weeds and by compressing $1/2$-inch gravel with a roller if you want to walk on it (see page 22).

Crushed stone is a cheaper substitute for natural gravel, but is difficult to walk on because of the sharp edges. Those edges, by the way, are sharp enough to cut a dog's foot pads. Beware of that fact if you have a pet.

Cobble is a large round-edged gravel from 1 to 10 inches in diameter and has many uses in the garden. It can be pressed into concrete, either close together, far apart, randomly, or in intricate decorative patterns. Cobbles are great as an edging for driveways, as a protective and decorative fill in a small planting area, or as an entranceway or driveway border. Laid close together in double or triple rows on either side of a concrete path, they give the illusion of running water.

Garden Hardscapes — Materials and Construction

Unfortunately, if you want to use cobbles in a driveway or for a path that receives lots of foot traffic, the cobbles will have to be set in concrete. Note: Keep the cobbles in a bucket of water until they are set in the poured concrete; dry cobbles absorb moisture from the concrete and will weaken it.

To lay the cobbles: First, see "Brick path" on page 25. After the concrete has been poured and leveled, press the cobbles flat or on end, depending upon the effect and surface that you require. Push them in far enough so they are firmly set in the concrete. Pack the cobbles closely together so only a minimum of mortar shows between them. Make sure the cobbles are level, then wash off any excess mortar. Do not allow anyone to walk on the surface for about 10 days.

If you are handy with tools, **wooden decks** are fairly easy to build. There are numerous detailed plans available in books that will lead you through their construction step-by-step. Wooden decks can be laid over gravel or other hardscapes as an added design element or as a raised staging area for garden furniture or potted plants. Wooden decks have a seasonal advantage over concrete or stone paving. In cold weather, paving can be uncomfortably cold to walk or stand on for any length of time. A wooden deck, on the other hand, tends to stay much warmer and dries quickly after a rain.

Water-Conserving Gardens and Landscapes

CHAPTER THREE

THE INSIDE STORY ON PLANTS AND THEIR NUTRITION

Adversity is said to be the mother of invention. In the plant kingdom, this truism is most obvious in those plants that survive under the harsh conditions of deserts and arid plains. Natural and hybrid species of such plants form the backbone of the water-conserving garden.

By understanding the basics of plant biology and by paying close attention to them, your gardening experience will be enhanced and your chances of success in the garden will be increased immeasurably. Let's start at the beginning.

Plants manufacture their own food (organic) from inorganic materials by photosynthesis. Photosynthesis is a process that utilizes chlorophyll in the leaves of plants to convert carbon dioxide, which is absorbed from the air, the water, and organic materials from the soil by the roots, into organic starches and sugars, amino acids, and fatty acids with the aid of the radiant energy of sunlight; during this process, the plants release oxygen. Without sufficient light, this process stops, and the plant will eventually die.

Germination is the beginning of plant growth from a seed or spore after its dormancy period. Most seeds remain dormant for varying periods of time, depending on the type of plant. Various affects may hasten germination, including different combinations of chemicals, moisture, heat, freezing, or scarification. (Scarification is the perforation of the hard seed coat with a knife, file, or sandpaper.)

Photosynthesis

The essentials for germination are viable seed, moisture, air, and favorable temperature. At germination, the shell or coating of the seed splits. A rootlet starts downward, and a sprout with one or more seed leaves pushes its way to the soil surface. The tip of the root consists of elongated cells that continually grow and push the roots deeper and farther out into the soil. Just behind the root tip is a zone of delicate, single-celled root hairs that absorb water and nutrients. These delicate hairs will quickly dry and shrivel if they are exposed to the sun or dry air, which is why seedlings must be quickly transplanted.

The stem of the plant, of course, supports the plant or tree. The stem is composed of conductive cells that pass water and nutrients up and down the plant and has special cells for food storage. That is why it is so vitally important not to tie wire or tight ties around the stems of plants.

The basic function of leaves is to convert carbon dioxide and

32

water into carbohydrates. With the aid of sunlight, the chlorophyll within the leaf acts on the carbon dioxide from the air and on the soil solution from the roots and manufactures sugar and starch — the basic food substances of plants. A by-product of this action is oxygen. Just 2,500 square feet of grass produces enough oxygen to support two adults and two children.

The solar-powered process of photosynthesis in leaves is not only ingenious and efficient, but also is a process that is vital to the survival of all other life-forms. Plants provide energy for the entire food chain, while they delight us with their form and beauty.

Finally, there are the flowers—the reward for the gardener. Most plants and trees produce flowers of some kind. Flowers are the plant's apparatus by which most plants propagate themselves. The flower contains male stamens that produce pollen and the female pistil where the seeds are produced. For the seeds to be produced, the pollen has to be transferred to the pistil either by wind, birds, insects, or mammals. While most flowering plants have both male and female reproductive parts, some plants have single sex flowers on the same plant or are single sex plants.

To ensure pollination, most flowering plants utilize scent, form, color, or all three to attract the attention of birds and insects. Once pollination takes place and fertilization occurs, the energies and food of the plant are concentrated on vegetative growth and seed development.

During a plant's development, it utilizes fifteen elements that are essential to its nutrition. Three of these elements are obtained by the plant from water or air — carbon, hydrogen, and oxygen. The remaining twelve elements are: boron, calcium, copper, iron, magnesium, manganese, molybdenum, nitrogen, phosphorus, potassium, sulphur, and zinc. These twelve elements are normally obtained by the plant from the soil, but minerals also can be absorbed through the leaves of plants; this is called foliar feeding.

Evidence of nutritional deficiency is not easy to detect. For example, slow growth, small leaves, or pale or yellowish leaves may indicate a need for nitrogen. Typically, the veins of the leaves remain a deep green color, while only the spaces between the veins of the leaves turn yellow or whitish. *New* growth, however, that is yellow or whitish may indicate an iron deficiency; this is called iron chlorosis.

The Inside Story On Plants and Their Nutrition

Iron chlorosis may occur in many soil conditions: in soil that is too salty (saline); in soil that is high in calcium; in soil that is too wet or too dry; or in soil that has not been deeply watered. The long-term remedy is to add organic amendments to the soil (see Chapter Four). For short-term correction, you can buy iron chelates to mix with the soil or for spraying on the leaves (foliar feeding). You can store iron for the plant in the soil by making a few holes several inches deep just outside the root zone and by putting 1 tablespoon of iron chelate in each hole.

A good fertile loam usually will provide all the elements that are needed for growth, but these can become depleted or not available to the plant for a variety of reasons. This is where fertilizers come into play. In arid soils, the addition of fertilizers usually is needed for healthy plant growth, but always remember to use small doses of fertilizer with low-water-use plants.

TYPES AND USE OF FERTILIZERS

There are three nutritional elements that are required by plants that are likely to be in short supply in soils that have not been conditioned recently with organic amendments or in areas where the land previously has been under cultivation. These elements are nitrogen, phosphorus, and potassium.

Nitrogen stimulates the growth of leaves and stems and is needed by plants in relatively larger quantities than phosphorus or potassium. Phosphorus accelerates maturity, helps with seed formation, and stimulates root growth. Potassium (potash) strengthens stem and leaf growth and generally helps to improve the health of the plant.

The most commonly used fertilizers today are inorganic; they are compounded from chemicals. Organic fertilizers, however, are being used by more gardeners everyday because they are safer for both the soil and the gardener. You may want to consider possible results of use before deciding upon inorganic or organic fertilizers. Widespread contamination of groundwater supplies by the nitrates in inorganic fertilizers has led to the closure of thousands of wells across the nation. If your drinking water source is your private well or a nearby community well, I definitely would advise the use of organic fertilizers.

Whether you use inorganic or organic nitrogen fertilizers, too much nitrogen in the soil can weaken the plant's cell walls and make it susceptible to disease. It also will cause the plant to grow more foliage at the expense of root growth; in drought conditions, that increases the plant's water loss into the air (transpiration) and reduces its water uptake, making the plant drought sensitive. Since plants need comparatively more nitrogen than the other two elements, phosphorus and potassium, care must be taken when choosing the nitrogen supplement.

Help Roots Break Out

When you dig a hole to plant a new tree, there is something else that you must do besides fill the hole with an organic amendment and fertilizer. Before planting, take a fork and break down the solid side walls and the bottom of the hole. If you do not, the new tree roots will eventually hit the hard side walls and bottom of the hole, turn back on themselves, and become root bound. Breaking up the walls and bottom of the planting hole will encourage the roots to spread out and down.

There are many inorganic nitrogen supplements on the market: nitrate of soda, calcium nitrate, ammonium sulphate, ammonium phosphate, Cyanamid, and urea. If you decide to use inorganic nitrogen, either by itself or in the commonly sold nitrogen-phosphorus-potassium mixtures, it must not be allowed to come in direct contact with plants because inorganic nitrogen burns the leaves and stems; if it accidentally falls onto leaves, spray the leaves immediately with a hose.

The traditional and environmentally-safe way of insuring a supply of nitrogen, phosphorus, and potassium (potash) is to grow cover crops of alfalfa, clover, soybeans, ryegrass, etc. Sometimes called "green manure," these crops usually are grown solely to be spaded or tilled back into the soil to replenish the soil with nutrients and organic matter. The home gardener can condition a vegetable garden or a planned orchard with green manures with wonderful results.

The most valuable cover crops are the legumes — clover, alfalfa, hairy vetch, and soybeans. If you decide to add nitrogen to your soil

35

by using legume cover crops, inoculate the seed with nitrogen-fixing bacteria, which are essential to the production of nitrogen; this bacteria can be purchased at your local garden supply store or through mail-order garden catalogues. Also ask your local seed supplier or nursery which legumes are suitable for your area and when is the best time to plant cover crops and to till them back into the soil. Usually gardeners plant cover crops in the spring and till them under in the fall so the plants have time to break down and release nitrogen over the winter months.

Other organic sources of nitrogen, phosphorus, and potassium (potash) are dried and aged manure, compost, cottonseed meal, and dried blood meal.

Inorganic sources of phosphorus, the second element needed for healthy plants, are superphosphate or concentrated (or triple) super-phosphate, which are natural phosphate rock sold either raw or acid treated. These can be purchased at your local garden supply store. Especially good sources for organic phosphorus supplements are raw or steamed bonemeal, rock powders, and fish meal.

The most common inorganic potassium (potash) fertilizer is potassium chloride. Other forms that are sometimes available in garden supply stores are potassium sulfate and the combined mix-ture of potassium and magnesium sulfates. If you decide to go the organic way, try wood ashes, greensand (glauconite), or cocoa shell meal.

Fortunately, you do not have to be a chemistry major to decide on a fertilizer. There are "complete" fertilizers available for general garden use that will serve the average water-conserving garden well, whether the fertilizer is for flowers, vegetables, trees, or shrubs. (Most low-water-use plants, however, may need phosphorus, which promotes strong root growth.) These complete fertilizers indicate on the bag the amount of nitrogen, phosphorus, and potassium (pot-ash). Most complete fertilizers available also contain the trace elements mentioned above. You can also purchase fertilizers that have been compounded for regional soil conditions; definitely ask about these specialized fertilizers at your local nursery.

Basically, if water, soil, and temperature are adequate, and the plant looks sickly, it is either a nutritional deficiency or an attack from a viral or bacterial disease or an insect or animal pest. Although many low-water-use or drought-resistant plants tend to be more resistant to nutritional deficiencies and parasitic invasions than many of their cultured cousins, these maladies do occur.

The most susceptible time for a plant is when it is young before it has had time to build up a strong root system and abundant foliage. Low-water-use plants are no different than other plants when they are young. They, too, require tender loving care at the seedling stage and during the first one or two years of growth (see page 12). Once mature, though, low-water-use plants require less attention, far less water, and usually less fertilizer than other plants.

TROUBLESHOOTING AILING PLANTS

When a plant is not doing well or gradually is going downhill, it takes a little detective work to find the true cause or causes. It could be that the soil is too acidic or too alkaline, or that salts have accumulated near the roots and need to be leached away with a deep, thorough watering; it could be that the plant cannot survive direct sunshine, or that the drainage is so poor that the roots are drowning from lack of oxygen; it could be that when the plant was bought, the roots were potbound and have grown in on themselves, or that the plant species is not suited for the environment. This is why choosing plants that have been proven to thrive in your locality is so important.

The speed with which a plant declines is a good clue. If it suddenly withers, then chances are it is one specific cause, possibly a pest or some form of root rot. If the plant declines over a period of time, chances are it is being stressed by the environment; usually there is more than one thing wrong.

Observation comes first. One day you notice that the leaves on your favorite plant are twisted and puckered. The first thing is to look for aphids, mites, or leaf rollers. To locate some pests, such as spider mites, and as an aid to seeing what is really wrong with a plant, you will need a magnifying glass. If you cannot see any insects, chances are the damage was done months earlier by thrips — tiny insects that suck the juice from leaves. As the leaves grow, they become distorted around the wounds, but the leaves are otherwise functioning, so take no action.

If you assume the damage is caused by an insect and try to eliminate it, you could be wasting your time. More important, you

37

Clues to Plant Problems

LEAVES	POSSIBLE CAUSES
Green *(normal shape, but undersized)*	Insufficient water Lack of nitrogen Zinc deficiency Nematodes on roots
Green *(normal shape, but wilting)*	Insufficient water Root rot or nematodes Poor drainage, roots drowning Too much fertilizer Grubs attacking roots Exposure to chemicals
Yellow *(normal shape)*	Nitrogen deficiency Normal aging
All brown *(normal shape)*	Normal aging Frost damage Insufficient water Twig borers or cicada damage Root rot
Brown on edges only *(normal shape)*	Frost damage Salt buildup in soil Herbicide damage
Center of leaf brown *(normal shape)*	Sunburn damage
Pale color *(new leaves have deep green veins)*	Iron (deficiency) chlorosis
Pale color *(all leaves have deep green veins)*	Soil too wet, poor drainage
New leaves mottled	Viral infection
Purplish color *(normal shape)*	Phosphorus deficiency Frost damage
Silvery look *(normal shape)*	Leaf hoppers
Bronze color *(normal shape)*	Red spider mites

38

Leaf edges chewed	Grasshoppers
	Beetles
	Birds
	Snails
	Crickets
	Caterpillars
Leaf edges ragged, torn	High wind damage
Leaf puckered	Mites
	Zinc deficiency
Semicircles cut in leaf	Leaf-cutting bees
Leaf chewed or gone, but stalks remain	Birds
	Rabbits
	Ants
All leaves gone	Rats
	BIrds
	Rabbits
	Squirrels
	Ants
Many leaves suddenly on ground in normal growing season	Frost
	Drought stress
	Fertilizer burns
	Birds

could be missing the real cause. There are still two other possible causes: one, a viral disease; two, the plant has been exposed to a herbicide.

Sometimes, especially with smaller plants, you will have to dig up the plant and inspect the roots. With larger bushes and trees, you will have to dig down and check the roots as they lie in the soil, causing as little damage to the roots as possible. The roots could be dried out, rotted, dead, twisted in on themselves, or could have been eaten by a gopher or borer beetles.

Sometimes you may find that the roots are covered with whitish bumps of varying sizes, usually in thick clusters. These bumps are most often caused by microscopic worms called nematodes. There are hundreds of species of nematodes, and some are specific to individual plant species. Suspect nematodes when there is no obvious insect problem, but the plant is stunted and does not respond to increased fertilization or watering. Unfortunately, there is no real cure for nematodes except very unhealthy fumigation of the soil. Plants that are infected have to be destroyed. Do not replant the area with the same species of plants. Try something totally different.

Books can help you become a better plant diagnostician (see page 135), but cannot replace practical experience. It can be very profitable to join your local gardening club or horticultural society where gardeners get together to discuss these problems.

Defenses Against Drought

Naturally drought-resistant plants have developed a number of ingenious survival mechanisms in order to live in deserts and other arid regions where water is extremely scarce.

Some plants, such as cat's-claw *(Macfadyena unguis-cati)* and asparagus fern *(Asparagus setaceus),* simply evade the water problem by going into dormancy. They wait until the temperature and moisture are sufficient to support growth, then they reemerge in a remarkably short time.

Some plants protect their leaves with a waxy coating or with thousands of fine hairs to reduce moisture loss. Leaves of some drought-resistant plants tend to be smaller and colored gray rather than green, white, or silver in order to better reflect the sun's heat; some leaves have the ability to turn away from the sun or fold into themselves.

An example of an old hand at drought survival is the mesquite tree *(Prosopis glandulosa torreyana),* which sinks a taproot deep into the soil (sometimes going down 200 feet) where groundwater accumulates. Even a small seedling of mesquite can be a serious problem to remove because it may be anchored with an 18- to 50-inch root. In the open desert, mesquite may never grow larger than a small shrub, but it becomes a large tree when water is readily available.

Many drought-resistant trees have modified the structure of their branches and leaves to minimize heat damage and maximize moisture intake. The palo verde tree *(Cercidium floridum),* for instance, has small leaves that do not absorb much heat and an open branch structure that allows rain or dew to collect and flow down the tree trunk to the shallow fiberlike root system near the soil's surface; it also has a long taproot that finds moisture deep below the surface.

40

Some desert plants also have developed extremely tough and penetrating root systems that drill through cementlike caliche or hardpan (see pages 53 to 56). Even rock does not deter the evergreen pistache tree *(Pistacia lentiscus);* it can penetrate rock by excreting a dissolving acid from its root tip.

The utilization of such hardy low-water-use plants in the water-conserving garden, together with healthy imports from other countries and the many hybrid species that have been developed for garden use, opens up a fascinating new world for gardeners to explore (see Chapter Seven for other plant suggestions). A world of plants that not only conserves precious water, but also performs this task in remarkable and divergent ways.

The Inside Story On Plants and Their Nutrition

CHAPTER FOUR

SOILS AND SOIL IMPROVEMENT

The Greeks called soil the base of all life. Modern gardeners call it dirt. Somewhere between this poetic reverence and disdainful slur lies the truth. Soil is a complex mass of mineral particles from the decay or weathering of the planet's crust that are mixed with living and dead organic matter, air, and water. Soil contains the minerals and the organic and inorganic chemicals that support plant life, together with the organisms and microorganisms that help plants break down and utilize all of these various elements. The nature of that soil — its heaviness or lightness, its chemical nature, its moisture and air levels, its acidity or alkalinity — determine the very nature of the plants that grow there.

The gardener has no control over the climate. Sunshine, rain, humidity, frost, and snow come and go as they please. But there is one area over which the gardener does have control — the soil in the garden. In controlling the condition of the soil, the gardener can exert a major influence over growing conditions and lessen the affects of adverse climatic events.

In the xeriscape garden, the control of soil conditions will repay the investment in time and effort many times during the life of the garden. One of the many advantages, however, of low-water-use plants, especially native species, is that they will usually survive in almost any soil; so do not despair if your garden soil resembles the surface of Mars. With low-water-use plants, you will be working with nature, not against it.

How to Rescue Neglected Trees

If you have bought a house with some sadly neglected trees, or if you have a tree that just is not doing well, there is a way to give the tree a boost. First make sure that the problem is not a disease or the result of a gopher that is eating the roots.

With a posthole digger, auger, or garden spade, dig a series of deep holes about 2 feet farther out than the drip line of the branches, all around the tree. The holes should be about 2 to 3 feet apart and at least 30 inches deep. Fill each hole with a mixture of compost, organic mulch or cow manure, ammonium phosphate, and sulphur. The proportions are roughly: 6 cubic feet compost (4 $1^1/_2$ cu.ft.bags), 2 pounds ammonium phosphate, and 3 pounds soil sulphur. Mix thoroughly, fill the holes with the mixture, and irrigate. Once the tree is back on its regular watering schedule, it will have an ample supply of nutrients to regain the lost growth.

Plants that are chosen for their suitability in the existing soil structure will be more successful and require less care than plants that are forced to adapt to the existing soil conditions. Plants are extremely adaptable organisms, but it usually takes more than one generation of plants for that adaptation to the soil environment to take place. Plant breeders gradually alter the soil conditions and environments over many generations to allow plants to adapt and grow in other areas. In the water-conserving garden or any other garden, plants that are selected for their compatibility with the existing soil structure will survive at less cost in terms of fertilizer, disease, and pest control; and they will be more successful.

In xeriscape gardening, plants and soil are "tuned" to produce a beautiful garden or landscape with the least possible amount of water. This "tuning" of the soil is accomplished with the same techniques that are well known to successful gardeners. Some techniques include the addition of organic soil amendments, such as ground bark, peat moss, leaf mold, aged sawdust, aged wood shavings, manure, or compost. There are also inorganic mineral soil amendments, such as pumice, vermiculite, and perlite to improve the texture, and lime and gypsum, which are used to improve clay soils and to alter the alkalinity of the soil.

Natural decay and bacteria turn soil amendments into humus, which is a soft brown or black substance that is formed in the last stages of decomposition of animal or vegetable matter. Humus binds together minute clay particles into larger particles that improve aeration and drainage. In sandy soils, humus fills in the pore spaces to help hold water and nutrients in the soil.

Soil Management

Soil management has been called the most fundamental component in gardening. Unless you have been fortunate enough to buy the property of a dedicated gardener, rarely do you find a soil that is ideal for cultivating plants. In most housing developments, the topsoil is usually scraped off to dig foundations or to level the site. This exposes hardpan — a tight, impervious layer of soil, which is called caliche in the Southwest. Or if the topsoil is spread back over the site, the use of heavy equipment at the site can turn the topsoil into hardpan.

The ideal soil for plants is called garden loam, which is a mixture of sand, silt, and clay, and is the most fertile environment for plants. Garden loam is porous enough to provide good drainage and aeration so that the plants do not "drown"; it is spongy enough to retain moisture for many days so that the roots do not dry out; it contains sufficient humus to encourage soil bacteria to break down the minerals and chemicals in the soil so that they can be absorbed by the plant; and it contains sufficient minerals and other elements that are needed for healthy plant life.

Where does soil come from? Initially when the planet was almost entirely rock, the action of air, water, and frost disintegrated the rock surfaces and created a mineral soil. When the first plants began to live on land, they added their decaying forms to the mineral soil and enriched it with the humus that other plants needed to grow. That same, basic process of rock surfaces disintegrating to create soil continues today. In areas of the world where there is little if any plant growth, the soil remains almost entirely mineral or sandy as it does in the desert. In forested areas, the soil is deep and rich in organic material. Between these two extremes are innumerable combinations of soil types: some are sandy, some are clay, some are heavy in minerals, some are acidic, some are alkaline, and some are peaty (almost entirely formed of organic matter).

45

Generally, soil types for gardening are classed according to their texture in three basic types: sand, silt, or clay. The type of soil is determined by the size of the soil particles: sand, 2 to $1/20$ mm; silt, $1/20$ to $1/200$ mm; and clay, less than $1/200$ mm.

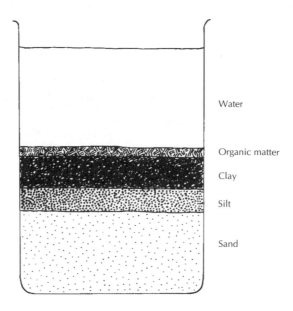

The importance of soil structure cannot be overemphasized: 100 square feet of sand will hold 60 gallons of water; clay holds 160 gallons, while loam will hold 90 gallons. An equal amount of water will be available to the plant and will penetrate only 4 to 5 inches in a clay soil, 6 to 10 inches in loam, and about 12 inches in sandy soil.

Fortunately you can improve the structure, fertility, and water-holding capacity of almost any soil. And when you do, you not only will gain the immediate rewards of a healthy, blooming garden, but also you will be contributing to the fertility of the planet for future generations.

There is a very simple test to determine the type of soil that you have in your garden. Take a handful of moist soil and squeeze it. When you open your hand, a good loam soil will remain a pliable ball that easily breaks apart with a touch of your finger. Good loam has a gritty feeling and is usually dark in color.

A fine clay soil will remain in a doughy, slippery ball when you open your hand. It feels smooth to the touch and sticky when wet.

After a rainfall or watering, the surface may bake into a hard crust that prevents water and air from reaching plant roots. Consequently, clay soil is difficult to work. While clay holds more water than any other type of soil, this is more of a liability than a blessing. Clay soil is very slow to dry out and slow to warm up in the spring. If it is worked while still wet, it forms hard lumps that are very difficult to break down. Clay is the most difficult soil type to manage, but with the addition of sufficient sand and organic amendments, it can be turned into loam.

A handful of moist sandy soil will form a shape when squeezed, but barely holds together. It feels harsh and gritty to the touch. Water drains through it very fast, but it dries out just as fast. Humus is needed to correct this condition. Sandy soils warm up fast in the spring and are easy to work. Without sufficient humus to hold the water in the soil, however, the soil dries out very quickly. Because of this fast drainage, soluble plant foods are lost through leaching. Adding lots of organic matter is the answer.

Loam is the best balance between clay and sandy soil. There is a balance between large and small particles; the soil is well aerated; it is easy to get moisture to the plant roots; and it does not dry out quickly. Loam is fertile and porous, has good drainage and aeration, and has sufficient humus to encourage the growth of needed soil bacteria.

Quick Soil Test

To quickly find out the composition of your garden soil, put 1 cupful of soil in a tall quart jar. Add 4 cups of distilled water and 1 teaspoon of Calgon or other dispersant. Shake the jar for at least 5 minutes. Put it on a shelf and let it settle.

About 5 or 6 hours later, the sand will have filtered down and will be resting in a layer on the bottom. A short time after that, the silt will form a second layer on top of the sand. Being so much finer, clay may remain in suspension much longer, but after 18 to 24 hours, the clay will also have settled to form a third layer. When the clay has settled, the water will be brownish in color, but almost clear. Measure the three layers with a ruler and calculate the percentage of each to find out if you have sandy soil, silty soil, or clay soil. Good garden loam has roughly 70 percent sand, 15 percent silt, and 10 percent clay.

47

In some soils, however, the texture changes as you go deeper. At the surface, a good loam or moderately sandy soil can sit on top of a layer of compacted soil or clay. This compacted layer will prevent drainage so that plants in the top layer will become waterlogged. The hard layer below can also prevent plant roots from reaching down to their optimum depth.

A quick way to check soil drainage is to dig a 2-foot-deep hole and fill it with water. When the water has drained from the hole, fill it again. If there is still water in the hole two days later, there is a drainage problem that will have to be solved by either drilling holes through the hard soil layer with an auger or by installing drainage tiles. If this drainage problem exists, though, in only one or two areas, it would be easier for you and better for the plants to build raised beds for the plants instead of drilling holes or installing tiles.

Remember that the maximum depth for plant roots is different for different plants. The roots will attain that depth only if the soil is moist and contains sufficient air and nutrients. In the water-conserving garden, you want your plants to send roots down to their maximum depth. Deep-rooted plants that have a greater reservoir of water and nutrients to draw from can survive longer between waterings and can withstand drought conditions far better than shallow-rooted plants. Information on how to ensure that moisture and nutrients reach deep-rooted plants, and how to test the soil for moisture penetration is given in Chapter Five.

In the water-conserving garden, annual beds usually will need to be about 10 inches deep; perennial beds and shrub borders will need to be from 18 to 14 inches deep. Why? Well, water drains away in soil through gravity. The moisture that is held in the soil by capillary action in the minute pore spaces between the particles of the soil keeps the soil moist and the plant healthy. The size and number of those vital pore spaces are determined by the structure of the soil itself. Garden loam consists of a mixture of clay, silt, sand, and humus that provides the optimum drainage, the optimum moisture and air retention, and the optimum environment for soil bacteria.

There is hope, though, for those who do not wish to invest the time, money, or effort to make the soil into an ideal environment; they can grow selective low-water-use plants that will thrive in poor soil (see Chapter Seven for plant selections). It just will take more time for the garden to grow to maturity.

SOIL AMENDMENTS

To change the condition or structure of soil requires the use of a lot of amendments — as much as 25 to 50 percent of the total soil volume in a given area. You have to add enough amendments to change the soil structure. If you are conditioning the soil to a depth of 12 inches, spread at least 3 to 4 inches of amendment (compost, peat, bark, etc.) material over the planting area and mix it thoroughly with the existing soil, either by spading it in or by using a rotary tiller. The type of amendments that you use, however, depends upon the existing soil structure.

Peat is the partially carbonized residue of plants. It is rich in organic matter, readily absorbs and retains moisture, and is relatively free of weed seeds and harmful fungi. Peat, however, is somewhat acidic, so it must be used with consideration to the pH level of the soil and the type of plants to be grown. Peat is usually sold in bales or in large plastic bags. Puncture the bale or bag and soak it well before opening; used dry, peat is very difficult to manage and will blow away in a light breeze.

Soil-Testing Procedure

Soil tests are conducted by state agricultural experimental stations, which are usually listed in the telephone book under the state Department of Agriculture. With a spade or trowel, dig a V-shaped hole about 6 to 7 inches deep. Take the loose dirt out and cut a thin slice of soil from the side of the hole. Take the sample from the top to the bottom of the hole. Spread the slice of soil to dry on a clean sheet of paper; keep it covered so that the sample is not contaminated with dust or chemicals.

When dry, pack the soil in a sealable plastic bag for shipment to the state laboratory. If you have two obviously different kinds of soil in the sample (sand in the top few inches, heavier soil below), separate the two soils for drying and pack in separate plastic bags. With the soil sample include the date when the sample was taken, how you took the sample, and how it was dried. Do not take the sample immediately after a heavy rain or watering because this will affect the nutrient levels in the soil.

49

Leaf mold is rich in organic matter and is able to change nitrogenous materials in the soil into a form that plants can absorb. A majority of leaves from deciduous trees are neutral or only slightly acidic. Oak leaves and pine needles form a leaf mold that is acidic. You can make your own leaf mold in a compost heap, or you can buy it at garden supply stores. If you can find it, the best leaf mold comes from the natural forest floor.

Wood products, such as ground bark, aged sawdust, and aged wood shavings, can also be used as soil amendments. The organisms that break down these organic materials need nitrogen. If they cannot get the nitrogen from the amendment itself, however, they will take it from the plants. Most of the organic amendments, such as bark, aged sawdust, peat moss, or leaf mold, that are bought at a nursery or garden supply store are nitrogen fortified. Raw wood shavings, raw sawdust, ground bark, straw, or manure that is mixed with straw usually require the addition of nitrogen. To add nitrogen to soil amendments, use 1 pound of ammonium sulfate for each 1-inch-deep layer of organic amendment that is spread over 100 square feet.

Compost is a blackish or brownish, crumbly material that results from the decomposition of organic products — leaves, wood ashes and chips, clippings, and fruit and vegetable refuse. Compost takes time and effort to make, but is well worth the effort. Decomposition takes from six weeks to six months, depending upon the way it is done. Entire books have been devoted to composting (see *Let It Rot!, The Gardener's Guide to Composting* by Stu Campbell, Garden Way Publishing, 1990), but the basic compost pile consists of alternating layers of organic-rich material, soil, and animal manure stacked about 4 feet high.

The pile should be turned once a week to distribute the heat and moisture that are at the center of the pile where decomposition takes place. Moisten the pile as needed to keep it slightly damp. Decomposition can be hastened with a few handfuls of fertilizer or a commercial compost activator. It is easier to hold the compost within some type of square or rectangular container that is made of slatted wood, wire mesh, or concrete blocks, etc., with an opening on the end for air to penetrate. A compost bin with three separate compartments works best because you can fork or shovel the material from one to another as it decomposes. New material is placed in the right compartment, partly decomposed material is transferred to the middle compartment, and fully decomposed material is shoveled into the left compartment, which is then ready for use.

Composting is a wonderful way to put your household waste to productive use. Compost can be used to improve the condition of the soil or can be used when planting seedlings, shrubs, vegetables, or trees. Screened compost makes a good mulch around vegetables and tightly packed flowers with delicate stems. Compost that is mixed with equal parts of water can be used as "compost tea" to water tender, new transplants and houseplants; compost that is mixed with soil

Compost Bin

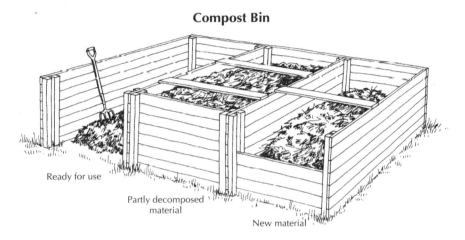

Ready for use

Partly decomposed
material

New material

makes an excellent seedling or plant potting mixture. In most cases, rich compost that is worked into the soil will be the only fertilizer that your garden needs.

ACIDIC VERSUS ALKALINE SOIL

The relative acid or alkaline level of soil is very crucial to plants. Some plants thrive in acidic soils, while others wither and die. Fortunately, most low-water-use plants prefer a neutral or slightly alkaline soil; many of them originally flourished in arid regions where the alkaline level of the soil was extremely high. The relative acidity or alkalinity of both water and soil is measured on a pH scale. The pH stands for potential hydrogen and is a scale that was developed by chemists. There are fourteen divisions on the pH scale, from

1, which is highly acidic, to 14, which is highly alkaline. A pH reading of 7 is neutral. Simple to use pH soil-testing kits are available at most nurseries and garden supply stores. Regular soil testing for pH is highly recommended.

For most gardens, a pH level of between 6 and 7 appears to be optimum, but soils can become slowly acidic or alkaline over a period of time, so twice yearly tests are in order.

Quick Soil pH Test

Professional soil tests can be expensive. A quick way to test your soil at home is to buy pH testing strips at a nursery or a pool store. The pH paper strips turn color when placed in water, and the color is matched to a chromatic chart which shows the pH level.

You will need a clear test tube or a small bottle with a stopper. Add distilled water and 1 or 2 pinches of soil to the test tube. Put the stopper on (do not use your finger as this will affect the pH reading) and shake the bottle. Let the mud settle to the bottom. Dip in a test strip and match it against the color chart.

If the pH is unusually high or low, you may want to make a more reliable test before investing in soil amendments. You can buy a soil-testing kit at a nursery or garden supply store. These kits contain a chemical that is added to a soil sample, and the resulting color of the soil is matched against a color chart.

The acidity of the soil can be changed by adding organic and inorganic amendments. To increase the acidity of an alkaline soil, the addition of acidic organic materials is necessary. The following amendments work well: oak leaf mold, rotting bark and wood from old logs and stumps of oak or hemlock, partly rotted sawdust from oak or hemlock, finely ground sphagnum moss, coarse, acid peat moss, or oak leaf mold.

To make acidic soils more alkaline, use lime. Lime in the form of ground limestone or hydrated lime not only corrects the acidity in soil, but also hastens the bacterial action and decomposition of

52

organic matter and helps to liberate plant foods into a form that plants can use. Spread the ground limestone over the ground and mix thoroughly with the upper few inches of soil. Do not spade or till it into the soil. **Caution:** Never mix lime with animal manure or nitrogen based fertilizers. The reaction releases ammonia that can kill plants.

Limestone must be used with caution, however, and in the quantities that are recommended on the package. Do not use more than 50 to 75 pounds of limestone per 1,000 square feet of soil at any one time. An excess of lime can cause severe iron deficiency in plants (see pages 33 and 34).

Soil conditioners are primarily sold for use with sticky clay soils. Gypsum and calcium sulphate displace the sodium that makes clay soil sticky and hard to work. Such conditioners, however, are of little use in sandy soil or in soil with a high proportion of organic material. (See the Source List on pages 149 and 150 for suppliers of soil amendments and conditioners.)

ARID SOIL CONDITIONS

Soils with a high alkaline content are common in many parts of the country. These soils break down into three main types: calcareous, saline, and sodic soils. All three types of soil can exist, however, in one location. Each of these soil types causes nutritional deficiencies in plants by not allowing iron, zinc, manganese, and other minerals to dissolve so that plants can absorb them.

Calcareous soil usually contains a high level of calcium carbonate. This is what forms the hardpan or caliche that is so dreaded by western gardeners. The hardpan is almost impossible to dig without using a pickax, and plant roots cannot break through it. Layers of hardpan can be up to 6 feet thick and are formed when rain or surface water deposits calcium from the surface to about 6 to 20 inches into the soil.

Caliche (hardpan) was laid down in the soil over many thousands of years as rain and flash floodwaters deposited salts and chemicals on the soil. In nondesert areas, these chemicals are mostly washed down rivers. In the desert, without rivers and ample rainfall, the chemicals penetrate the soil and accumulate in layers. These layers of hard minerals and chemicals are the reason that vast, shallow lakes can be seen in the desert after a heavy rainstorm. The caliche prevents the water from draining through the soil; it also presents an impenetrable barrier to deep-rooted plants. If your plant's roots reach caliche one or two years after planting, they will stop there. Water that collects on top of the caliche will drown the roots by denying them oxygen. It will also expose the roots to deadly levels of salts because your irrigation water and fertilizer will stop at the caliche, and salt buildup will occur.

Caliche can be ¼ inch thick or 5 feet thick, but the results on your plants are the same. So, you have to know where the caliche is and remove it. If you plant a tree without digging a large enough hole, caliche can prevent the tree from establishing a secure root system. During a heavy wind, your tree may blow over. This happens frequently in desert gardens.

Before spending a lot of money on soil amendments and fertilizer, first find out the depth of the hardpan. The best way to do this is with a soil probe — a 3-foot metal rod with a handle on one end. A ½-inch diameter rebar, which is sharpened at one end, makes an excellent probe. To determine the depth of caliche, wet the ground so that the soil probe pushes easily into the soil. When the probe reaches caliche, it will stop. Draw a map with graph paper with each square representing 3 or 4 square feet of ground. Record how deep the soil is in each square.

If you have 2 feet or less of soil above the caliche, the caliche has to be removed. If the caliche is 1 inch or less thick, it can be broken up quite well with a pickax or crowbar. If it is thicker than 1 inch, you will have to dig down and remove it, then replace the soil.

Digging through caliche is very difficult. The technique is to chip away with the pickax, then put about 6 inches of water on top of the caliche. Do something else for a few hours (dig another hole for another tree) to allow time for the water to soften the caliche, then chip away again. Repeat until you are through the caliche layer. Use a crowbar to pry up the caliche slabs so that you can remove them. For trees and large shrubs in hardpan soil, dig planting holes much deeper and wider (5 feet deep and 5 feet wide) than you would ordinarily.

At least 3 feet of soil is needed for most garden plants for the roots to grow and for vital drainage. Test the drainage before planting because plants will die if waterlogged. Pour 4 inches of water in the

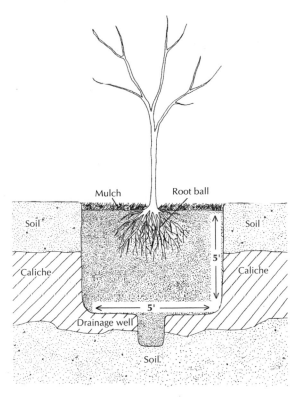

Mulch
Root ball
Soil
Soil
Caliche
Caliche
5'
5'
Drainage well
Soil

Planting a tree in an area where caliche is present requires a 5'x 5' hole. When caliche is thick, dig a 1' diameter drainage well or "chimney."

bottom of the planting hole. If it does not drain away in 3 to 4 hours, dig or drill drainage holes with an auger several feet deeper than the bottom of the planting hole. If the water still does not drain away, choose another location or plant a tree that can survive in hardpan or caliche soil, such as mesquite *(Prosopis glandulosa torreyana)* or palo verde *(Cercidium floridum)*.

If you have a deep hardpan layer, raised bed gardening is highly recommended. In raised bed gardening, you ignore the existing soil and create beds of new soil that are raised above the level of the ground.

55

Alternatively, consider planting trees in large containers where you can accurately control the soil conditions, fertility, and moisture levels. Large and attractive concrete containers are available from commercial landscape suppliers. You also can build your own

Soils and Soil Improvement

Sterilizing Soil Without Chemicals

Sometimes an area becomes so infested with weeds or with undesirable pests, such as nematodes, verticillium wilt, various root rots, pill bugs, and others, that trying to grow anything becomes a losing battle. In this case, the answer is to sterilize the soil.

Chemical sterilization, however, is too drastic. The chemical poisons the ground, sometimes for years, and if it migrates from the area as it often does, it will kill other plants and trees.

There is a way to sterilize soil by using clear plastic sheeting and the sun. First clear away all dead plants and other debris, including twigs and stones that could tear the plastic, add any needed soil amendments, and rake the surface smooth. There are two ways to do the next step. The first technique is to then irrigate the soil so that it is saturated at least 18 inches deep and lay clear plastic sheeting over the area. Use bricks or stones to firmly hold down all the edges of the plastic. Leave in place for 1 month. Then remove the plastic and dig up the ground to expose lower areas of soil to the heat. Replace the plastic sheeting for another month. At the end of this time, you can prepare the soil as needed and set out your plants.

The second technique, which is used at the Theodore Payne Foundation, Sun Valley, California, is to carry out the same procedures as the first technique but wet the soil only to a depth of 1 inch and lay down the clear plastic sheeting. At the Foundation's native plant nursery where this procedure is used, the most effective results are obtained where average high summer temperatures range *above* 90°F for 6 to 8 weeks. This procedure will not be successful in areas with regular summer overcast or moderately warm temperatures. (See the Source List on page 145 for address.)

containers with concrete blocks or with sections of large diameter sewer pipe that are cut to size.

Saline soil is overloaded with soluble salts, such as sodium chloride. It is often seen as a white crust on the surface of the soil after groundwater has evaporated. A similar crust can form in the bottom of the planting hole and burn the plant roots. Periodic deep waterings are needed to leach out these salts below the root depth of the plants. Large quantities of gypsum that are worked into the soil can help

Water-Conserving Gardens and Landscapes

considerably, but if the problem is very severe, get expert help in conditioning the soil from your local agricultural extension agent.

Sodic soil contains too much sodium in relation to calcium and magnesium. Such soil is also known as alkali, black alkali, or slick spot soil. The pH is above 8.5 and when wet, the soil often becomes dark in color with a slick, slimy surface. With sodic soils, the soil structure has broken down and has no air spaces to allow roots to grow; moisture cannot drain through it. Again, large quantities of gypsum are in order, but since this type of soil often contains other soluble salts, a soil analysis and some expert help are indicated.

Soil salts are the bane of arid soils that are found in the Southwest or in highly irrigated land where commercial crops have been grown. The salts tend to accumulate in layers at the surface of unbroken subsoil. Since water cannot drain into the subsoil, it stands in pools. The solution is to break up the subsoil before planting anything and to wash away the accumulated salts with repeated, deep soakings.

The above is by no means all there is to know about soil. By their very nature, low-water-use plants tend to be more highly tolerant of poor growing conditions than traditional high-water-use plants, but these basics on soil improvement will help you to have a successful water-conserving garden. A word of caution: Even though mature low-water-use plants are extremely hardy, all plants require care and nurturing during their first season of planting in order to build the deep root systems that allow them to survive conditions that are fatal to most other plants (see sidebar on page 12).

Soils and Soil Improvement

CHAPTER FIVE

WATERING — WHEN AND HOW MUCH ?

Some gardeners can tell at a glance, others examine leaves and stalks with their fingers, some push a steel rod into the ground, while others use moisture meters. Most of us, however, develop a kind of intuitive feeling about when to water the garden.

There is, of course, the simple and most obvious indicator of when to water. For centuries, gardeners have just looked at the top 3 to 4 inches of soil. If it is dry, chances are that you need to water, especially if it is the growing season. This test applies to all soils in all climates, but it does not apply necessarily to the water-conserving garden.

The water-conserving garden uses drought-tolerant plants that can survive very well in the top 3 or 4 inches of dry soil as long as the roots can obtain some moisture. Also, the xeriscape garden is characterized by the use of mulches to cover the soil, by the extensive use of decks, walkways, and other hardscapes, and by the recommended use of drip irrigation that delivers water to the root zone. Consequently, that centuries-old test could be wildly inaccurate.

The essential hardiness of drought-resistant plants will give you plenty of leeway for any possible mistakes in watering far more than in a conventional garden where water-demanding plants may show signs of collapse and wilt if you forget to water them for more than one or two days.

To organize and to carry out a precise watering schedule can be confusing since there are so many variables: the nutritional and watering needs of each individual plant during each season, the age of each plant, the nature of the soil, the weather (temperature, wind, humidity), and the method of watering. It can be sorted out, though, with a little effort, and the results will be very worthwhile.

Light watering   Deep watering

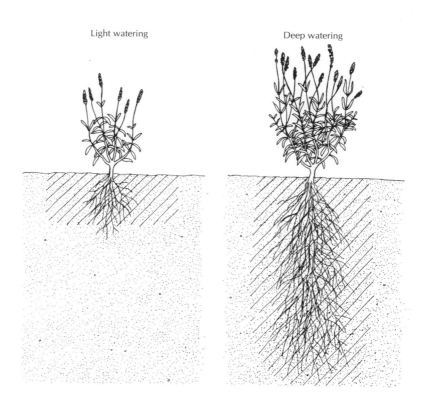

In the water-conserving garden, the primary concern is for sufficient water to reach at least 60 percent of the plant's root zone. The roots of plants need water, air, and nutrients to survive and grow. If you only water the top 12 inches of soil, then the roots will only develop in that top 12 inches. Shallow watering keeps the roots shallow and exposes the plant to serious damage if the weather turns very hot or if you forget to water the garden. Deep watering, however, permits the roots to penetrate to where they can tap into deep moisture reserves in the soil and enables the plants to survive hot spells or a missed watering. Many low-water-use plants are extremely deep rooted; this allows them to endure long periods without water.

Water-Conserving Gardens and Landscapes

Water moves down through the soil through progressive wetting of the soil particles. It takes a long time for moisture to penetrate 2 or 3 feet into the ground, which is why drip irrigation is so effective. The emitters on a drip system can direct the water to the root zone, so it is not necessary to soak the surrounding ground (see Chapter 6 for more information on the drip irrigation system).

The first step in setting up a watering schedule is to ask the supplier of your plants for recommendations on watering times. The supplier should be familiar with local soil conditions and with the drought-resistant plants that are sold in your area. Use this advice as a guideline to set up your watering schedule, then adjust the schedule up or down as your experience dictates. Taking into account the type of soil, the type of plants, and how much water per hour your irrigation system delivers, turn on the water system for as long as you think is appropriate. Evaluate your success by taking soil moisture samples from different areas of the garden.

Soil-Sampling Tube

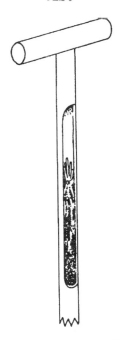

Take a soil moisture sample with a soil-sampling tube. This is a tube with a serrated bottom edge and a T-bar handle. The tube has a cut-away portion so you can see the soil sample without having to push it out of the tube. The tube is pushed into the ground, then twisted out. Do not push the tube too close to the plant, or you could damage the root ball. If the soil core is moist for only the first few inches and you know that the plant roots go down at least 12 inches, the watering time needs to be increased at least 3 to 6 times longer. Most soil-sampling tubes are 10 to 21 inches long, but you can get

A hollow tube pressed deep into the ground removes a core of soil. A side of the tube is missing so that you can also use this tool to observe roots, soil types, etc.

Watering — When and How Much?

extensions for some models that will give you a core sample of up to 3 feet deep.

Some gardeners use a metal rod about a ¼ inch in diameter with a handle to check the moisture level in soil. You also can buy a 3-foot-long lawn sprinkler handle that is available at most hardware stores for a few dollars. Cut off the prongs of the sprinkler handle and sharpen the bottom end. The rod will push through moist soil fairly easily, but when it reaches dry soil, it will stop.

For large containers or raised beds, a simple moisture probe can be made from a stake of light-colored cedar, redwood, or balsa wood, about a ¼ inch round and sharpened at one end. Push the stake into the container and away from the main root ball; leave it in the ground for a few moments, then take it out. The moisture will darken the stake. For small containers, a pencil with the varnish or coating removed works well.

MOISTURE SENSOR GAUGES

Moisture sensor gauges are far more sophisticated soil-sampling devices. Several types of moisture sensors are available, both automatic and manual. Automatic sensors are wired into the control box in an automatic irrigation system. These sensors override the timer and make the automatic irrigation system far more water efficient.

I like the idea of soil moisture sensors and automatic controllers, but without them I grew five acres of ornamental shrubs, trees, annuals, perennials, a vegetable garden, and fruit trees with a simple drip-tubing system that was attached to outside faucets. I determined the water schedule by walking around and looking at the plants. If they looked or felt dry, I watered them. With sensors and electronic controllers or timers, I probably could have done a much better job and could have saved more water, but even with my crude drip irrigation system, I cut the water bill (in my case the electrical bill to run the well pumps) by 40 percent when compared to the former system of sprinklers, hoses, and flood irrigation.

If you like having everything totally under control or do not have too much time available, then by all means go the automatic route. You will get great results with minimum water use and a minimum demand on your time.

Water-Conserving Gardens and Landscapes

Moisture sensors use different methods to measure moisture. Tensiometers, for example, measure soil moisture content and vacuum and normally are used as permanent fixtures in the garden.

Tensiometers

If you do not have automatic controls on your irrigation system, tensiometers can still be permanently located in the garden; simply check the reading on the meter to determine when to turn on the water.

For fully automatic operation, wires connect the tensiometer to the control box or valve of the irrigation system. There is an adjustable, magnetic switch that is mounted over the pressure gauge. When the needle goes past the moisture level setting that you have chosen, the magnetic switch activates the control box or valve to start the watering cycle. In this way, the tensiometer can tell the control box to skip certain, preprogrammed watering cycles if the soil moisture is adequate. Watering cycles also can be shortened and can save water since the tensiometer will shut down a watering cycle once sufficient moisture is indicated in the soil.

The controller or timer on the irrigation system must be programmed differently, though, when using automatic moisture sensor control. The controller or timer is set to water the maximum number of times available. In this way, the controller or timer continually checks with the sensor before activating. Only if the soil is dry will the watering cycle go forward.

The number of moisture sensors you use is up to your budget and how many different water-demand areas you have. With drought-resistant trees and shrubs, you may not need to use a moisture sensor, but for ground covers and shallow-rooted ornamental plants and vegetables, they can be invaluable. To have a very economical setting, set the sensor to its lowest moisture level reading and watch plants for the first signs of moisture stress; then reset the switch so that the watering cycle starts just prior to the first stress signs. Stress signs to look for: leaves that lose their luster, that become a dull green

63

color, or that take on an abnormal, gray or blue appearance. Do not wait until the leaves wilt because the damage to the plant may be severe.

Other moisture sensors include a manual, portable tensiometer, which is a sealed, water filled, metal tube. With a sample tube that is supplied, you take a core sample from the soil and then put the sensor tube into that hole. The end of the sensor has a porous, ceramic tip. Leave the tube in the ground for about 5 minutes. The gauge will register the partial vacuum that is created as the soil draws water from the tube through the ceramic tip. The drier the soil is, the higher the moisture tension is against which plant roots must pull in water from the soil — the drier the soil, the higher the reading on the gauge.

Electronic moisture sensors are now available. One type measures soil moisture through moisture pressure and temperatures; another measures the level of hydrogen (a component of water) in the soil. For extensive landscape areas or orchards, there is a system of electronic moisture snoops called marshmallows — marshmallow-sized gypsum blocks that contain electrodes. Check with your garden supply retailer as to their availability in your area.

WATER-SAVING MULCHES

A great deal of water in the soil is lost through evaporation, particularly in hot, dry climates. The value of mulch in the garden is well known. Mulch helps to prevent weeds; insulates the soil from temperature changes; keeps the roots moist and cool; extends the period between waterings; keeps the soil cooler in the summer and warmer in the winter; prevents valuable topsoil from drying out and blowing away; and protects delicate plant stems. Organic mulch, such as aged sawdust or shredded and chipped bark, even encourages earthworms to remain in the topsoil to enrich it and keep it well aerated.

In the water-conserving garden, mulching plays a decorative as well as a practical role. By their nature, many low-water-use gardens tend to be less "dense" and more spread out than the lush water-demanding plantings in conventional gardens. Mulch, therefore, becomes an important decorative aspect of the water-conserving garden design and can make a dramatic visual impact in addition to saving valuable water.

64

Do Not Let Rain Get Away

For thousands of years, people have collected rainwater and stored it in cisterns for use in dry seasons. Rain barrels that were outside homes were in common use during much of this century. With the rising cost and scarcity of fresh water, collecting rain is an idea whose time has come again.

One woman in an area where the average rainfall is only 16 inches yearly collected 5,000 gallons from a 400-square foot roof. She collected the rainwater in a 5,000-gallon pool that was 15 feet in diameter and 4 feet deep. This pool was connected to a drip irrigation system that operated by gravity feed from the pool.

Other ideas for reservoirs include vertical, plastic pipe tanks placed alongside the house and painted to blend in with the building (10 feet of 18-inch polyvinyl chloride (PVC) pipe holds 132 gallons of water). The PVC pipe costs about $7 a foot, and the end caps cost about $30 each. An outlet in the bottom feeds water by gravity to the irrigation system. Used aboveground swimming pools also make good reservoirs. They can be bought very cheaply; often for nothing, if you take it down and cart it away.

Remember, your roof must be rust-free, noncorrosive, and not painted with a lead based paint. Insert some type of T-junction or other means of choosing whether rainwater from downspouts goes to storage or in the ground. This will allow you to let the first fall of rain wash the roof and eaves of dust and debris before diverting the rain to storage. A removal filter on the downspouts and at the outlet of the storage container will keep out leaves and other debris that can turn the stored rainwater "sour." It also will reduce the risk of blockage in your irrigation system.

Rainwater also can be used to leach out salts in small container plants. Submerge the plant in the pot in a bucket or barrel of rainwater for a few minutes; repeat several times, allowing the water to drain away each time.

65

All manner of materials have been used for mulches, including compost, animal manures, leaves, leaf mold, aged sawdust, rice hulls, cottonseed hulls, sand, stones, gravel, wood and bark fragments, and shredded newspapers. Black plastic sheeting also conserves moisture and cuts down on weeds. Also available is a polypropylene landscape fabric that is permeable to water and air; its primary purpose is to stop weeds from growing. Covering this fabric with a thin layer of organic mulch improves the appearance and slows down the degradation of the plastic by sunlight.

Gravel, for example, when used as a mulch is well suited to xeriscape gardens. Whether you use gravel for a mulch or for decorative purposes, underlay it with plastic sheeting. The plastic will prevent weeds and discourage rodents. Use a gardening fork to

One way to use landscape fabric is to lay the fabric first, hold it in place with wire prongs, and set the plants in place through slits that are cut in the fabric. The fabric is then covered with organic mulch.

Water-Conserving Gardens and Landscapes

perforate the plastic sheeting with small holes to allow rainwater to seep away; then put down the gravel. Do not place gravel or small stones, however, near a grown tree; you will be removing leaves continually from the gravel. Use chopped wood bark instead; it tends to blend well with tree litter. Or grow a drought-resistant ground cover, such as juniper *(Juniperus horizontalis* cvs.*),* that tends to hide fallen leaves and twigs. Do not allow gravel or stones to touch plant stems because the reflected heat from the sun will burn the stems.

The most commonly available mulches at nurseries and garden centers include shredded or chopped wood bark, which is natural looking and decomposes slowly, but does turn gray after exposure to the sun; aged sawdust, which does not steal nitrogen from the soil as fresh sawdust does; aged redwood dust, which is long lasting; decorative bark, which needs to be 3 to 6 inches deep to be effective and tends to blow away in windy areas; peat moss, which is acidic and when dry, repels moisture and can blow away; and commercial compost, which usually is nutrient-rich sewage sludge that is mixed with wood by-products. Be aware that this sludge contains contaminants, such as heavy metals, especially cadmium. If you question government figures on safe contaminant levels, use organic mulch.

Read the label on the bag of mulch, or ask the salesperson if the mulch is composted or is a mixture of partially composted materials. Composted materials are decaying plant or animal material; as they decompose in the soil, they improve its structure. Noncomposted materials, such as fresh wood shavings or fresh sawdust will decompose and condition the soil, but will rob your plants of needed nitrogen. If you use noncomposted material, apply a controlled release nitrogen fertilizer by mixing about 3 pounds of fertilizer to 1 cubic yard of noncomposted mulch. Partially composted material, such as manure, contains high levels of salts that can damage plants. Do not use partially composted material in the spring and summer; it can be used in the fall, so winter rains can wash out the salts before spring.

Mulching is mostly common sense. Since mulch acts as an insulator, do not apply mulch to the garden until the soil has warmed up in the spring. The best time to mulch is following a good spring rain. In the fall, mulch will keep the soil warm, protect it from overnight frost, and extend the growing season.

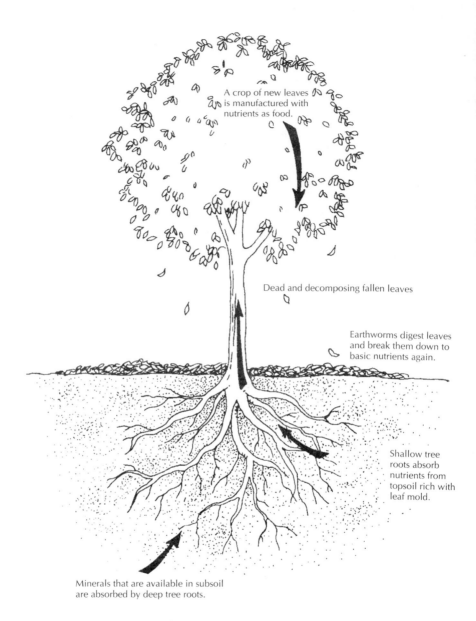

A crop of new leaves is manufactured with nutrients as food.

Dead and decomposing fallen leaves

Earthworms digest leaves and break them down to basic nutrients again.

Shallow tree roots absorb nutrients from topsoil rich with leaf mold.

Minerals that are available in subsoil are absorbed by deep tree roots.

Leaves in any state of decomposition make excellent mulch. They contain many of the essential trace mineral elements that the long penetrating tree roots have retrieved from the subsoil. In addition to the basic nutrients that all plants need — nitrogen, phosphorus, and potassium — leaves also have minerals, such as boron, cobalt, and magnesium.

Water-Conserving Gardens and Landscapes

CHAPTER SIX

LOW-WATER-USE IRRIGATION

Most gardeners water their gardens and landscape with oscillating sprinklers, pulsating sprinklers, or a simple hand-held garden hose or watering can. All of these irrigation methods are viable and mostly efficient, but there are some definite disadvantages with their use.

1. Overhead watering can result in a loss of up to 30 percent or more of the water to runoff and evaporation.
2. Overhead watering usually uses about 45 percent more water in order to *deeply* water landscape plants.
3. Overhead watering in some plant locations, such as hilly areas, may wash away valuable topsoil.
4. Overhead watering may promote fungal disease in plants by creating a too moist environment from wet plant leaves.
5. Overhead watering is very time consuming.

Drip irrigation, however, is the most efficient irrigation system that you can select for your xeriscape garden. It can save as much as 70 percent of the water that is dispensed by hoses and conventional sprinkler systems in the average garden. With a drip system, runoff and water that are lost through evaporation and overspray can be eliminated, regardless of how irregularly shaped or steep your property happens to be. Drip irrigation can be adapted to almost any garden situation: orchard or vegetable gardens, rooftop or patio gardens, large or small planting beds, or just a few containers. (Trickle irrigation is similar to the drip system, but water is released at a faster rate to avoid clogging the system; this eliminates the need for a filter and is often used where the water supply contains a lot of particulate matter.)

One of the key benefits of drip irrigation is that it can maintain nearly perfect moisture levels in the root zone of plants and can eliminate the too wet/too dry variations of overhead watering. The result is healthy fast growing plants. Very little water is lost to evaporation, and walkways and areas between plants remain dry, which reduces weed growth. This makes for easy cultivation even while watering is taking place.

Drip irrigation uses $1/2$-inch or $3/8$-inch flexible polyethylene pipe tubing. It is easy to cut with pruning shears or a knife, and all the fittings (T fittings, L fittings, couplings, end caps, on/off valves, etc.) are compression fittings that do not require gluing. A complete, garden drip irrigation system can be laid out by one person in a few hours. The water is delivered to the plants through emitters, which are various push-in or screw-in devices that are designed to deliver water by drip or minispray at a predictable rate and at a wide variety of water volumes to suit any plant or soil condition.

A modest investment will give you a hassle-free irrigation system that will pay for itself in water and labor savings in the first season. The systems that are available today at most nurseries and garden supply stores combine simple and sophisticated components that together can handle almost any watering situation. Control can be either manual or via a digital automatic controller, so you can accurately program watering time and duration if you are away from home.

GROUP YOUR PLANTS

One of the basic rules of water-conserving gardening is to group plants according to their water needs. This, of course, simplifies the irrigation system since all the plants in a particular area will need approximately the same amount of water. For plants that do not need *regular* watering, you could use a temporary soaker hose or a root irrigator attached to a garden hose. Drip irrigation, however, does make it possible to have plants with different watering needs closer to each other than with conventional irrigation. You simply use low gallonage emitters on the plants that need less water and high gallonage emitters on the plants that need more water. Make sure there is enough space between the plants so that water from the higher water use plants does not spread out far enough to "drown" the lower water use plants.

The simplest drip system consists of one long polyethylene pipe tubing that snakes through the entire garden and connects to a single water valve. You can use higher output emitters, or you can double up on the number of emitters for plants that need more water. In practice, though, it is much better to set up multiple systems with plants with similar water needs on the same system. Large plants, such as grown trees, then can receive the deep watering that they require, while less water-demanding, shallower-rooted plants can receive more frequent but less deep watering.

The various irrigation lines can be left aboveground, but if you have lots of open spaces or deck areas, they can be buried in the soil or covered with mulch. If you keep the soil or mulch cover no more than 2 inches wherever there are emitters, a wet spot will show aboveground so that you can check if the buried lines are working properly.

Another excellent way to run irrigation lines beneath hardscapes or decks, particularly the pliable polyethylene pipe tubing of drip irrigation lines, is to lay a section of oversized, rigid PVC (polyvinyl chloride) water pipe to carry the irrigation lines beneath the hardscape. Be sure to use a thick-walled PVC pipe.

DRIP IRRIGATION SYSTEM DESIGN

Estimating the type and number of emitters, connectors, valves, and other fittings is much easier and more accurate if you sketch the irrigation system to scale on graph paper. The system is best designed by starting with the location of each plant and the number and type of emitters that are needed. (See the section "Drip Irrigation Equipment" on pages 74 to77, including chart.) Then sketch back toward the water source. You then can quickly tell if the system exceeds the water delivery of the outside faucet or tap to which you are going to attach the system.

You can roughly determine the maximum water delivery of the water source by running the water at full force into a measured bucket; time how long it takes to fill the bucket. For instance, if it takes 30 seconds to fill a 5-gallon bucket, then the maximum water delivery from that tap is 10 gallons per minute or 600 gallons per hour. Manufacturers recommend that systems be designed to use no more than 75 percent of the outside faucet or tap capacity as a safety margin for water pressure fluctuations.

The first time I used drip irrigation, I was in a hurry to put a system in for a row of Arizona pines that ran the full length of one side of a five-acre parcel. I thought I could eyeball the system, so I ran out the $\frac{1}{2}$-inch polyethylene main supply line and secured the end of the line with a rock (it takes one or two days for the line to unwind and lay flat). I then punched a hole in the line at each tree, pushed in a short length of $\frac{1}{4}$-inch microtubing and snapped the barbed end of the emitter into the microtubing. After two or more hours on my knees in the sand, it was all done. I turned on the tap and was happy because from now on I would not have to drag around heavy hoses to flood irrigate the trees.

The system worked wonderfully for the first one hundred feet, but the pressure dropped dramatically from that point on. By the time the water reached the last ten or twelve trees, it had been reduced to a barely perceptible trickle. The solution was to divide the system in half with two separate water sources. So I do recommend that you spend a little time planning the system and determining if the water pressure is sufficient. This may not be a problem, though, for those on a municipal water supply.

Changes in gravity and friction are the two key factors that affect water pressure. Running a line uphill will reduce water pressure, while running a line downhill will increase water pressure. The friction that is generated by water against the inside walls of the tubing reduces pressure, and the longer the system is the greater the pressure loss. Friction loss increases at higher water flow rates and in smaller tubing sizes. For flow rates of below 100 gallons per hour, use $\frac{3}{8}$-inch polyethylene pipe tubing; for flow rates up to 320 gallons per hour, use $\frac{1}{2}$-inch polyethylene pipe tubing. Half-inch polyethylene pipe tubing costs about $12 to $13 per 100 feet, approximately $50 for a 500-foot roll. The price for $\frac{3}{8}$-inch polyethylene pipe tubing is about $8.50 per 100 feet and $34 for a 500-foot roll.

When you unroll the pipe tubing, it tends to keep its shape, so you have a series of half coils, which make accurate measuring difficult.

Water-Conserving Gardens and Landscapes

The best way to stretch out the pipe tubing is to place the coiled tubing close to the water source for the system that you are laying out, pull the tubing from the roll, and walk the end of the tubing to where the system will end. Place a rock or heavy object on the end of the tubing because it will curl back on itself. Leave it in the sun for 1 or 2 hours. The tubing will unwind, and you can then handle and snake it around the plants as you would a garden hose because the tubing will lie flat. Then cut the tubing from the roll.

If you are using emitters that are inserted directly into the $1/2$-inch or $3/8$-inch main supply line, then wait 1 or 2 days for the tubing to unwind fully. If you insert the emitters right away, some will be pointing at the sky and some will be pointing at the ground as the tubing unwinds. If you are going to use $1/4$-inch microtubing for emitters that are placed some distance from the main supply line, this is less of a problem. It will look neater, however, if you let the tubing unwind; this simplifies inspection for blocked or missing emitters.

With drip irrigation, if you run short of tubing, push one end of the tubing into a compression adapter and cut another piece of tubing to reach the water source. No glue or waiting is needed. The same procedure applies to adding extensions for new plants or additional garden areas. Simply cut the tubing, insert a T fitting or in-line connector, and add new tubing.

Occasionally you should flush out the system to remove any debris or bugs. End caps for the pipe tubing have a screw-on cap. Take the cap off, turn on the system, and flush for a few minutes, then screw on the cap. Many gardeners do not use end caps, but simply bend the poly pipe tubing and tie it with wire. This is a serviceable and leakproof way to end the system.

Years ago, microtubing was used extensively to place emitters at each individual plant. Besides making the system look like a giant centipede, the microtubing was quite fragile since it was easily ripped out by children, dogs, or cultivation. It is now much simpler and safer to run the larger main supply line tubing in and around the plants and attach emitters directly to the main supply line. Microtubing now is best used to deliver water to containers and hanging plants since it is much easier to conceal than the larger tubing.

Drip Irrigation System

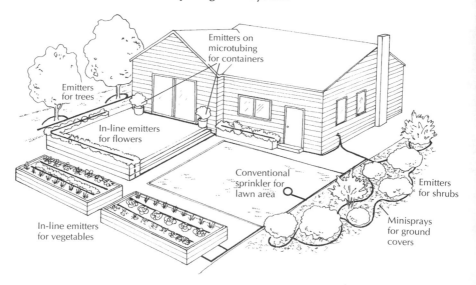

Emitters on microtubing for containers

Emitters for trees

In-line emitters for flowers

In-line emitters for vegetables

Conventional sprinkler for lawn area

Emitters for shrubs

Minisprays for ground covers

DRIP IRRIGATION EQUIPMENT

There are a number of manufacturers of drip irrigation equipment. Sometimes their equipment is interchangeable and sometimes not. There is a wide variety of emitters, minisprays, and misters to deliver water at rates that range from ¼-gallon per hour (GPH) to 2 GPH. The type of plant and the condition of the soil are the two factors that determine the number and type of emitter(s) that should be used. Generally, high gallonage emitters should be used for trees or for plants in sandy soil; for shallow-rooted plants or plants in clay soil, low gallonage emitters should be used. (See the chart on page 76 for a guide to emitter selection.)

Emitters come in three basic types, but all deliver water at a slow rate through small openings; they gently drip the water onto the soil. Emitters are best suited for individual plants and trees because the water placement is much more precise than with minisprays.

Turbulent-flow emitters ($.30 to $.40 each) have a larger water passage to minimize clogging that makes them useful if the water supply is of poor quality. These emitters have a twisting passageway that creates turbulence in the water flow and reduces the pressure to compensate for the larger opening; this makes them partially pressure-compensating.

Diaphragm-type emitters ($.30 to $.65 each), also called pressure-compensating emitters, use a pressure sensitive diaphragm to keep the water flow consistent despite water pressure changes. Some are self-flushing, others can be unclogged with a paper clip, and some have bug caps. (Some insects crawl inside emitters and sometimes clog the line if the water flow does not flush them out.) Do not use diaphragm emitters if your water pressure is below 5 pounds per square inch pressure (psi) or if the emitters, which usually operate between 10 and 50 psi, will not open. Diaphragm emitters are best suited for slopes and hilly terrain or on long irrigation lines with many emitters. If you use nonpressure-compensating emitters on such lines, uphill emitters will be fed less water, and on long lines, the emitters toward the end of the line may receive no water.

Vortex emitters ($.30 each) have an interior chamber that spins the water to a lower pressure. Some have a stem in the outlet that can be turned to stop water flow. High levels of calcium in water, though, will eventually clog most emitters, especially vortex emitters.

Most emitters have a barbed end that snaps into a small hole in the 1/2-inch or 3/8-inch polyethylene pipe tubing. You can buy a small ring punch for $2.00 that cuts the precise size hole in the wall of the tubing. For a few dollars more, there is a punch with an ejector button to stop the punch bit from getting clogged with waste plastic. You want to avoid having small bits of waste plastic fall into the main supply line where they can clog the emitters. (I have lost punches and used a two-inch nail to punch holes and have not noticed any difference in efficiency.) Be careful not to punch through both walls of the tubing. Even if a line is cut, it takes only two or three minutes to repair it with goof plugs, which are little plastic plugs that snap into the main supply line tubing and seal it completely. These plugs allow you to easily and quickly change the location of emitters in the main supply line or to add additional lines of microtubing as plants grow or the garden design changes.

If you wish to reach out further to other plants without running the main supply line to them, you can insert 1/4-inch polyethylene microtubing into the main supply line, cut this microtubing to the desired length, and insert an emitter in the end of the tubing.

EMITTER SELECTION

The plant and soil types determine the number and type of emitter.

Plants	Soil	Emitters	Placement
Low shrubs (1 to 3 feet)	Clay	One ½-GPH	Beside plant
	Loam	One 1-GPH	Beside plant
	Sand	One 2-GPH	Beside plant
Shrubs and trees (3 to 6 feet)	Clay	Three ½-GPH	Evenly spaced 6 to 12
	Loam	Two/Three 1-GPH	inches from stem
	Sand	Two/Three 2-GPH	or trunk
Shrubs and trees (6 to 12 feet)	Clay	Four ½-GPH	Evenly spaced on loop
	Loam	Two/Three 1-GPH	around shrub or tree
	Sand	Four 1-GPH or two 2-GPH	
Larger trees	Clay	Three/Six 1-GPH	Evenly spaced on loop
	Loam	Three/Five 2-GPH	around tree
	Sand	Four/Eight 2-GPH	
Flower beds, vegetables, and shrubby ground covers	Clay	Two/Three ½-GPH }	18 inches apart in each row
	Loam	Two/Four 1-GPH	
	Sand	Two/Four ½-GPH	12 inches apart
Ground covers and dense mats	Clay	½-GPH	Overlapping minisprays
	Loam	1-GPH	Overlapping minisprays
	Sand	2-GPH	Overlapping minisprays
Containers	Potting soil	One or several ½- or 1-GPH according to pot size	

Water-Conserving Gardens and Landscapes

For hedges and large vegetable beds, you can buy a drip line with factory installed emitters that are spaced 12 inches apart to deliver an even band of water. These lines can take rough handling and light foot traffic. Various flow rates, spacings, and pressure-compensating emitters are available; the cost is about $31 per 100 feet.

Emitters come in different colors (green, brown, black, etc.) to indicate the flow rate, but not all manufacturers use the same color code. Consequently, I would advise you to buy all the emitters for your irrigation system from the same manufacturer.

Misters ($.50 to $.90 each) deliver a very fine spray, which is ideal for ferns and similar plants that require high humidity and frequent watering. One mister will usually handle one or two plants, depending on their size.

Minisprays ($.40 each) usually come in 90°, 180° and 360° patterns, and in a 30° to 35° strip pattern. They usually are attached to plastic stakes ($.30 to $.75 each) that push into the ground and hold the spray at the desired height. They are very useful in tight corners or irregular spaces where you can match the spray patterns to the exact area to be covered without wasteful overspray.

Minisprinklers ($.75 to $1.50 each) spray larger areas and at a slower rate than minisprays. Available only in a full width 360° pattern, they are less affected by the wind than minisprays and will cover areas from 10 to 30 feet.

A wide variety of fittings are available for drip systems and range in price from $.15 each for microtubing couplings to $.55 each for ½-inch couplings. T fittings, L fittings, couplings, end caps, thread-to-tubing adapters, hose-thread adapters, and on/off and shut-off valves range from $.55 to $1.95 each. (See illustration on page 78).

Regulators, filters, and injectors are the main components of the head assembly — the components that are placed between the valve of the water source and the drip tubing. You can, of course, save money by not using pressure regulators, filters, or in-line fertilizer injectors. Just connect the drip tubing to the tap or main water valve and make sure no one turns the valve wide open, or the water pressure will blow the emitters out of the tubing. This method works, but when something goes wrong, you will wish that you had spent the extra money for a good filter and pressure regulator.

My first drip system worked well for a few months under this primitive setup, but the emitters were clogging at an annoying rate

77

Drip Irrigation Fittings

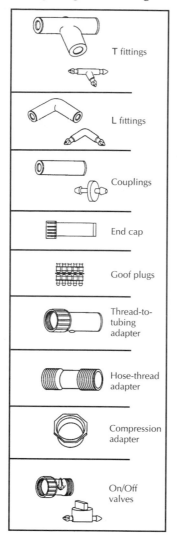

T fittings

L fittings

Couplings

End cap

Goof plugs

Thread-to-tubing adapter

Hose-thread adapter

Compression adapter

On/Off valves

since my well was liberally supplied with calcium, other mineral salts, occasional sand, and after three months, small plastic pieces. When one of the plastic blades on a modern well pump cracks or chips, it shreds the plastic into small specks and $1/8$-inch to $1/4$-inch filaments. All of these small pieces went into my holding tank and down the drip lines where they lodged in the emitter holes.

Even after flushing the lines, little strips of plastic kept clogging the emitters. I spent weeks inspecting the various drip lines, taking off the emitter and blowing out the plastic, or poking it out with a paper clip. It was not until much later that I found out that Y filters were on the market. A good Y filter would have saved me weeks of work.

If your water supply is fairly clean, you can buy a hose-thread filter for $5 that will handle a maximum flow of about 189 GPH. Check your household tap filters for evidence of sand, rust, and mineral deposits because these will clog emitter holes; if this is the case, use a Y filter on the head assembly (see illustration on page 83). It has a large filtration area and costs about $14 for a unit that will handle up to 6 gallons per minute (GPM); larger models with a flush valve will handle 8 to 20 GPM at a cost between $25 and $55.

Most home water systems operate about 45 to 100 pounds psi. Most drip irrigation systems are designed to run best at between 20 and 30 pounds psi. Using water at a higher pressure reduces the life expectancy of the system and increases the chances of fittings and

Water-Conserving Gardens and Landscapes

tubing blowouts. Most municipal water supplies are designed to deliver from between 50 to 100 pounds psi, and in some areas may range as high as 300 pounds psi. This amount of pressure can destroy a drip irrigation system. Therefore a pressure regulator is recommended for each drip system.

Pressure regulators are preset at 20 to 30 pounds psi and cost between $6 and $10 each. Preset inline pressure regulators cost about $5.75 for small volume, simple drip systems; for larger volume systems, there are inline pressure regulators preset at 20 to 30 pounds psi.

Drip systems that are connected to the household fresh water supply also need backflow preventers or anti-siphon valves to prevent water in the irrigation lines from siphoning back into the household water lines. This is **very important** if you plan to use a fertilizer injector on the system to deliver soluble fertilizer while watering. A simple hose-thread backflow preventer that screws onto a regular garden faucet costs about $3 or $4. The familiar plastic, manual anti-siphon valves that are found on most inground sprinkler systems also can be used on drip systems and cost about $13. As with all backflow preventers, the anti-siphon valve must be located higher than the drip irrigation head assembly to prevent the possibility of backflow into the main water supply.

The conventional way of spreading fertilizer over the soil works quite well with conventional overhead watering where the fertilizer is dissolved into the soil. What works well with drip irrigation is a fertilizer injector, which is basically a container filled with either a liquid or water soluble fertilizer.

The fertilizer injector is attached to the drip line *after* the anti-siphon valve or backflow preventer and *before* the pressure regulator. Water directly carries the dissolved fertilizer to the plant root zone without fear of burning and with practically no waste. A small, cartridge-type inline fertilizer costs about $9, while the bigger injectors (1 pint, 1 quart, and ½-gallon size) cost from $20 to $45 each. Note: If using dry, granular fertilizer, blend it with water before pouring it into the injector. The pint-sized ejector empties after about 50 gallons of water flow has passed through, while the ½-gallon ejector empties after about 150 gallons of water flow. With multiple drip systems, it is easy to disconnect the filter and to reconnect it to another system.

Inexpensive In-line Fertilizer Injector

If you do not want to spend the $20 to $45 for an in-line fertilizer injector cartridge, you can use a plastic gallon jug. You only need to buy a hose proportioner — a small brass fitting that screws onto the outside faucet or tap. A hose or dripline screws into the end of the hose proportioner. Attach a rubber tube, about ¼ inch diameter, to the small nipple on the fitting and put the other end of the tube in the gallon jug. Make sure that the tube is all the way inside the jug. Fill the jug with water and add 1 cup of water soluble fertilizer.

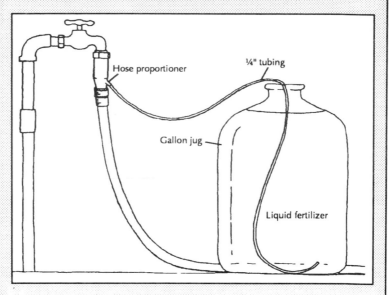

When you turn on the water to the hose or irrigation system, fertilizer will be drawn from the jug by the suction of the water flow in the hose or line. Plants will receive the equivalent of about 1 tablespoon of fertilizer per 1 gallon of water. You can adjust the strength to suit your plants' needs and fertilizer strength.

The advent of automatic irrigation controllers is a tremendous boon for busy home owners and their plants. It does away with the "Oops, I forgot to water the garden"; it allows home owners to go away on weekends or on vacation without having to worry about the plants; the plants are watered when they need it; and if the irrigation system

Water-Conserving Gardens and Landscapes

is set up properly, overwatering and underwatering become a thing of the past.

The simplest and cheapest controls are the battery operated timers, such as the Rainmatic 2000 Water Timer that attaches to the main water valve and controls one irrigation system. It can be programmed to turn on the water from once a week to four times a day and costs about $45. Also available is the Gardena 2030 Water Computer at $70, which can be programmed to turn on and off from once a week to six times daily.

For multiple drip irrigation systems, you can use an individually programmed battery operated controller for each system. If you can afford it, I would suggest that you use the more permanent controller systems. These consist of a solid-state controller that runs on 110 volts and is connected to automatic solenoid valves with a fine gauge valve wire. These timers lower the household voltage to a safe 24-volt supply that operates the automatic solenoid on/off valves. Most controllers come with a plug-in transformer so that an electrician is not required. The control box is usually designed to be mounted indoors. A small 1/4-inch hole that is drilled through the wall of a garage or utility room is sufficient to pass the multistrand wire to the solenoid valves. The number of strands that are used depend on the number of valves or systems that you have, plus one common strand. For example, with three valves in front of the house and three valves at the back, you would run a four-strand wire to each location. Each valve has two wires; one attaches to its own strand of the control wire, the other to the common strand.

Typical of lower-priced controllers is the HR 4000. It is solid state, controls up to four valves with a 0- to 99-minute running time per valve, and has a rain "off" switch and a plug-in transformer. The watering program is set by punching keys on the controller face, and the cost is about $40. The HR 6100, which costs about $90, controls up to six valves and has two independent watering programs. Independent watering programs allow you to program shallow, frequent watering for ornamentals and longer, deeper waterings for trees.

Even more flexible automatic controllers control from six-to-eighteen different valves or systems. The Oasis Koala-T Series, for instance, has plug-in modules so that the controller is expandable as your irrigation system grows. The basic four-to-six station controller will cost about $222 and $362 for the eighteen station model.

Automatic solenoid valves, such as those found on conventional sprinkler systems, cost about $18 to $23 each, while the valve wire will cost from $.13 per foot for two-strand wire to $.33 per foot for seven-strand wire. Valve wire is heavily coated and can be buried underground without the use of a conduit. When you run the wire, think ahead to how you may expand the system and run as many extra strands as you think you will need in the future.

THE COMPLETE ASSEMBLY

Now that we have looked at all the various components and accessories, how do they fit together? Ask your drip irrigation system supplier to lay out all the accessories in the order that they will attach to the water source; then check that you have all the required fittings to assemble all the parts of the drip irrigation system. Also draw a quick sketch of the complete assembly, or make a list of the parts in the correct assembly order.

If you are using an outside faucet or tap as the water source, first screw in the anti-siphon valve (vacuum breaker or backflow preventer), then screw in the hose thread filter. If you are using a Y filter, attach the Y filter with a ³/₄-inch fitting that is available from the dealer. Next attach the pressure regulator, either preset or adjustable, and finally attach a ³/₄-inch to ³/₈-inch (or ¹/₂-inch) thread-to-tubing adapter to which the drip irrigation tubing is attached.

If you are attaching a fertilizer injector, attach it immediately *after* the anti-siphon valve and *before* the filter. Note: Some fertilizer injectors have a built-in anti-siphon feature or vacuum breaker.

The same procedure applies when using an automatic solenoid valve and an automatic controller, except that most solenoid valves are equipped with an anti-siphon feature. If not, place the anti-siphon valve immediately *after* the solenoid valve. It is not always practical to place anti-siphon-type valves higher than the drip system; in hilly terrain, for instance, the solenoid valves may be below the elevation of the irrigation system.

If your area is hilly, add an independent anti-siphon device or vacuum breaker after the solenoid valve. Remember, the fertilizer injector always goes *after* the anti-siphon valve and *before* the hose thread filter or Y filter.

With drip irrigation, you can expand the system, shorten it, or reroute it with very little bother. It does, however, require visual

Drip Irrigation Head Assemblies

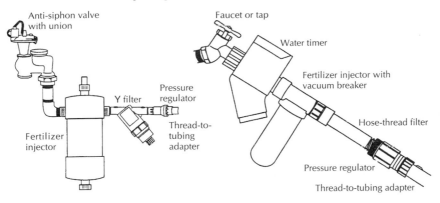

inspection from time to time. Emitters get clogged; plants grow and obscure minisprays; dogs, children, or careless cultivation sometimes knock out emitters. If you have very hard water that contains many minerals, you may need to inspect the emitters at least once a week. In the desert, when I checked the emitters, I carried a pocketful of emitters and a paper clip to clean out the emitter. If the emitter could not be cleaned easily, I replaced it and took the clogged emitter to the house for cleaning. Soaking the emitter in vinegar will remove the calcium scale that may accumulate inside it.

In the winter, even during hard frosts, water in the system that froze never caused a problem. The sun, acting on the polyethylene pipe tubing, melts ice very quickly. Since the tubing is flexible, freezing will not crack it as it will with rigid PVC fittings and pipe. End caps, T fittings, L fittings, solenoid valves, and other rigid fittings will crack, however, during heavy frost. To insulate these fittings and accessories, I have had great success with the spongy plastic sleeves that are used to insulate water pipes. Cut small pieces of the spongy material to fit around outside faucets or taps, fittings, and end caps; then wrap them with waterproof tape. For awkward T fittings and other odd shapes, patch bits of the spongy plastic around the fitting and secure with waterproof tape.

83

Special Plantings

Drip irrigation is especially useful in special planting situations, such as with plants that grow between paving or in a rock garden, where you can use a combination of drip emitters and minispray

Low-Water-Use Irrigation

emitters, depending upon individual plant needs. Other special plantings include the following.

Container plants. Drip irrigation is a boon for container plants, whether in the garden, along driveways, or on a porch. Under- and overwatering are the biggest killers of potted plants, but with drip irrigation you can accurately size the emitters to the pot size. If you put the system on an electronic timer, you can spend time away from home without worrying about your outside potted plants.

The usual setup is to run a $1/2$-inch or $3/8$-inch polyethylene main supply line below or behind the plants with $1/4$-inch feeder lines to each container. The main supply line can be hidden easily beneath a porch or deck railing. One $1/4$-inch feeder line can supply up to 10 emitters using T fittings to run emitters to individual plants.

Emitters are available with flow rates that range from $1/4$ gallon per hour up to 2 or more gallons per hour. In larger containers, you will need to place several emitters because of low, lateral water spread in potting soil (how far the water spreads out in the soil), which is usually not more than a 6-inch spread. Flow rates through $1/4$-inch feeder lines should not exceed 10 gallons per hour; for smaller, $1/8$-inch individual plant feeder lines, water flow should not exceed 4 gallons per hour.

Trees. The slow, deep irrigation that is possible with drip irrigation encourages tree growth, but does not encourage weed growth or leave pathways wet and soggy. The water requirements of trees, especially low-water-use trees, change with the seasons and the maturity of the tree. With drip irrigation, these changing needs can be easily accommodated. Start saplings with one emitter at the base of each tree, for instance, then add additional emitters as the tree grows.

If you have a row of trees to water, you can run a $1/2$-inch or $3/8$-inch polyethylene main supply line down the row of trees and place two emitters at the base of each tree. Even better is to run four emitters that form a square beneath the drip line to promote even root growth; alternatively, you can run two main supply lines on either side of the trees with two emitters from each line. A common setup, however, is to run one main supply line, then use a T fitting to add a loop of the main supply line with multiple emitters around each tree. This ensures even watering and growth of the roots. In sandy soils, you can use a minispray or sprinkler to cover the entire root area, but you

Water-Conserving Gardens and Landscapes

will lose more water to evaporation from sun and wind.

When designing your tree watering system, design it for the water flow that will be required when the trees are fully mature.

Vines. Difficulties that are encountered with the watering of grapes and other vines are solved with drip irrigation. One of the problems with commercial grape irrigation, for instance, is that many vineyards are built on hillsides, and conventional irrigation washes valuable topsoil away. When grapevines become wet from overhead or sprinkler-type irrigation, it promotes the growth of an unwanted mold to which grapevines are especially susceptible.

With drip irrigation, the main supply line can be tied to a wire that is suspended about 18 inches from the ground. The wire is attached to the grape stakes. At this height, the tubing sits above the area where cultivation and weeding is done. If you utilize this system for vines or other climbing plants, such as peas and beans, do not attach the emitters to the main supply line right away. Tie the polyethylene pipe tubing to the stakes and then allow the tubing to "unwind" for a few days (see page 73). Once the poly pipe tubing has unwound, emitters that are punched into the bottom surface of the tubing will stay pointed to the ground.

Vegetables. Most vegetables are water intensive because they thrive under continually moist soil conditions. With drip irrigation, however, water use can be reduced substantially.

For row vegetables, you can use the same $1/2$-inch or $3/8$-inch polyethylene main supply line and lay it between the rows; install emitters about every 12 inches or buy a polyethylene feeder line with in-line emitters that are already installed.

For widely spaced plants and for plants with deep root systems, such as tomatoes (up to 10 feet deep) and melons and cantaloupes (up to 5 feet deep), a single emitter can be placed at the base of each plant. When placing emitters, take into account lateral water spread — how far the water spreads out and down into the soil. In good loam, a $1/2$-gallon emitter will generally water an area 16 inches in diameter. For coarser sandy soils, use a 1-gallon emitter for greater lateral water coverage.

For intensive bed vegetable gardening, set the drip system up on a grid with feeder lines spaced about 16 inches apart and with emitters spaced every 12 inches. A bed that is 4 feet wide, for instance, will receive full water coverage from three feeder lines. You also can buy a porous

85

feeder line that gives a continuous band of surface moisture, rather than use individual emitters. Many gardeners report a 10 to 15 percent increase in vegetable production after switching to drip irrigation.

CONVERTING AN INGROUND SPRINKLER SYSTEM TO DRIP IRRIGATION

If you have a conventional sprinkler system in your garden, converting it to drip irrigation is relatively simple.

If you have more than one sprinkler line, install the pressure regulator and filter at the main water valve. If there is only one sprinkler line, you can install the regulator and filter either at the main water valve or on one of the sprinkler risers. Drip irrigation lines can run up to 100 feet from one riser outlet, so choose the riser that is best placed to cover the area. If you need to use two or more risers in different areas of the garden for full coverage, install the regulator and filter at the main water valve.

To install the regulator and filter at the main water valve, remove a section of pipe below the anti-siphon valve. Depending on the setup, you may have to dig down and expose the pipe that lies below the anti-siphon valve. Leave the anti-siphon valve in place. Either unscrew the vertical pipe from its elbow or L fitting or cut the pipe, whichever is easier. Then install the pressure regulator and filter.

There are fittings available to size the regulator and filter to your existing pipe. To ensure that you get the correct fittings, you can measure your sprinkler pipe and bring the regulator and filter to the hardware store. Once they are installed, remove all the sprinkler heads except the one or two that are to be used for the drip system. Cap the remaining sprinkler heads by using end caps and plastic pipe cement.

Attach a threaded elbow fitting to the sprinkler riser or risers that you are going to use for drip irrigation and wrap the threads with a nonstick fluorocarbon tape. You can buy fittings that adapt from the elbow to a compression fitting for the drip line tubing. It might be wise to glue these fittings in place.

If you are running only one drip irrigation line from a riser, attach the pressure regulator and filter directly after the elbow on the riser, insert the tubing for the main supply line, and lay the line where you want it.

You also can buy high pressure emitter heads that screw directly onto the risers without the use of an elbow fitting. These are fitted with multiple outlets for microtubing. They are designed for use with risers that are surrounded by clusters of plants, such as a border of perennials or shrubs. Microtubing does not work well if the plants are spread out because the tubing can be accidentally dislodged by someone walking nearby or by children and pets at play.

There are two key aspects to remember about low-water-use irrigation: The first is to deliver the correct amount of water at the right depth and in the right location to maintain a plant in a healthy condition; the second is to reduce moisture loss through evaporation and the drying action of the sun and wind with mulching (see Chapter Five). The overall dictum in water-conserving gardening is very simple: Water infrequently, but water deeply.

Low-Water-Use Irrigation

C H A P T E R   S E V E N

LOW-WATER-USE PLANT SELECTION

T he xeriscape landscape concept was initially prompted by the continuing and growing water shortage problem in the West. Naturally enough, it is in the West where the concept has spread most rapidly. The rising cost of fresh water, however, in the whole nation makes it of interest to home owners and professional landscapers everywhere.

Some of the plants that are described in this chapter can live through cold winters, but others cannot, such as the succulents — cacti, ice plant, aloe, etc. Fortunately, hardiness zone maps that cover the entire nation are readily available, and commercial plant growers label their plants with the hardiness zones that are suitable for each plant. Hardiness zones indicate the approximate range of average annual minimum temperatures. Within each region or state, however, more detailed climate zones maps are available through county extension offices, libraries, and most nurseries or garden supply stores. These climate zone maps are your guide to what will and will not survive in your area.

A little preliminary study of these climate zones will greatly increase your success, and a thorough understanding of microclimates in your own garden will enable you to successfully grow plants that are not usually considered suitable for your general climate zone. Although many of the plants that are described in this chapter are those that have grown well in states where drought tolerance has always been a factor, a good number of them have species or hybrids that are suitable for harsher winter climates.

When to Plant

The best time to introduce low-water-use plants is in the fall when the air is cooler, and the soil is still warm; the plants will have all winter to grow strong root systems. Drought-resistant plants need those winter months of lower light levels. At this time, the soil has more water to nourish the root systems that will carry the plants through possible dry years.

The relationship between roots and soil is far more important with low-water-use or drought-resistant plants than it is for ordinary garden plants. Good soil drainage is a must for these plants because wet, warm soil breeds diseases.

If you give low-water-use plants the chance to establish themselves properly with occasional deep watering during their first winter and summer, most of these plants will survive on rainfall alone by the second year. If conditions are not favorable, such as poor soil conditions and extremely hot, dry summers or dry winters, they may require watering during their second or third summer. In areas of very low winter rainfall, they may require watering once or twice during the winter. By the time these plants have tripled in size, you can begin to reduce watering.

If you are planting a completely new garden, the fall is the best time to landscape with low-water-use plants. If you are renovating your garden or are planning to change to these low-water-demand plants in stages, you can introduce the plants gradually. Preferably you can start with slow growing trees and shrubs and can spread the work and expense over several years.

How to Recognize Quality Plants

Shopping for plants is no different than any other kind of shopping. You want quality and value for your money. Does it look good? Is it the right color? Will it last? With plants, check to see if the leaves are healthy. When buying deciduous plants, especially shrubs or trees in containers or root balls, the bark should feel smooth when it is rubbed with the thumb; the branches should be pliable; and the buds should be plump and not shriveled looking. Check for healthy buds along the stem that will grow into branches; these can become damaged during transportation or handling. With conifers, the foliage should be full and should have new, brighter

Tips on Buying Container-Grown Trees

When buying a tree in a container, you want a well-developed root system. When trees have been grown in the ground, then dug up and put into a container for sale, early growth of the tree will be retarded.

A tree that has grown in a container has fibrous roots that fill out to the sides of the container. These fibrous roots hold the soil together in a compact mass. (If the tree has recently been put into the container, the soil will fall away when you lift the tree out of the container.) These small fibrous roots should be firm and white to pale brown in color. If they look dark brown and soft, they may have been burned when the sun heated the container. Most gardeners leave tree planting until the fall for many reasons; one of them is that trees newly shipped to the nursery in the spring are put into containers. By that fall, the trees will have survived the summer, and their root balls should be generous and healthy.

Do not buy a tree with a large diameter trunk that is grown in a small container. If you look on the bottom of the container, you will see roots that are sticking out or even buried in the soil below. Do not buy it. It is too old and undoubtedly rootbound.

If the tree is tied to a stake, closely inspect the ties. They should be made of stretchable plastic. If a sapling is tied too tightly to the stake, there is sometimes a sudden fattening or outgrowth of the trunk where the stake ends. If the damage is not severe, loosening the ties as the tree grows will correct it. If not, the tree trunk will be scarred and the cells that conduct nutrients will be damaged at that point. Never use wire, string, or any nonstretchable material as a plant tie. Inspect the ties regularly during the growing season.

green growth, which shows that the plant is not stunted or sick. Do not buy conifers with scanty, dull-colored foliage or those plants with branches too far apart; those branches will never fill out.

If by chance your local nursery owner is unfamiliar with the terms "low-water-use or drought-resistant plants," the name of the plant and the color, shape, and texture of leaves can be used as a guide.

Before the hundreds of drought-resistant plant species became

Low-Water-Use Plant Selection

readily available at nurseries, gardeners that were interested in such plants and in native wildflowers would roam the countryside and gather seeds or take clippings. You can do this, but be aware that many native plants are protected by law as endangered species. Take, instead, a few seeds or a small cutting, but not the entire plant. Your best option, however, is to contact a nursery that specializes in native plant species. They will have a fund of information about the cultivation of local wild plant species. (See the Source List on pages 145 to 148.)

Most drought-resistant plants share a number of common features that you can use to single them out from their water-demanding cousins. Hairy-leaved plants are usually drought resistant, as are those with silver, white, or gray leaves. With many of these pale-leaved plants, the leaf itself is green but the dense coating of hairs gives them a pale white, gray, or silver cast. Popular low-water-use plants with hairy leaves include lavender *(Lavandula* spp.); the French *(L. dentata)* and Spanish *(L. stoechas)* lavenders are less water demanding than the well-known English lavender *(L. angustifolia)*. Others include rosemary *(Rosmarinus officinalis)*, various daisy species *(Chrysanthemum* spp.*)* and *(Erigeron* spp.*)*, woolly yarrow *(Achillea tomentosa)*, the wormwoods *(Artemisia* spp.*)*, lamb's ears *(Stachys byzantina)*, and the fragrant thyme family *(Thymus* spp.*)*. Aromatic herbs are a favorite for both fragrance and color in the xeriscape garden since most of these herb species are drought resistant.

As you can see from a glance at the following low-water-use plants, these plants have a tremendous array of colorful flowers and interesting foliage. Your water-conserving garden can look as colorful and appealing as an English garden (see pages 110 and 111), or it can capture the flavor and romance of a Spanish adobe patio garden with the sagelike, gray-blue hues and the fragrance of lavender *(Lavandula* spp.*)*, fern-leaf tansy *(Tanacetum* spp.*)*, cushionbush *(Calocephalus brownii)*, Matilija poppy *(Romneya coulteri)*, viper's bugloss *(Echium)*, santolina *(Santolina* spp.*)*, and sage *(Salvia* spp.*)*.

92

Water-Conserving Gardens and Landscapes

Regional Guide to Plant Selection

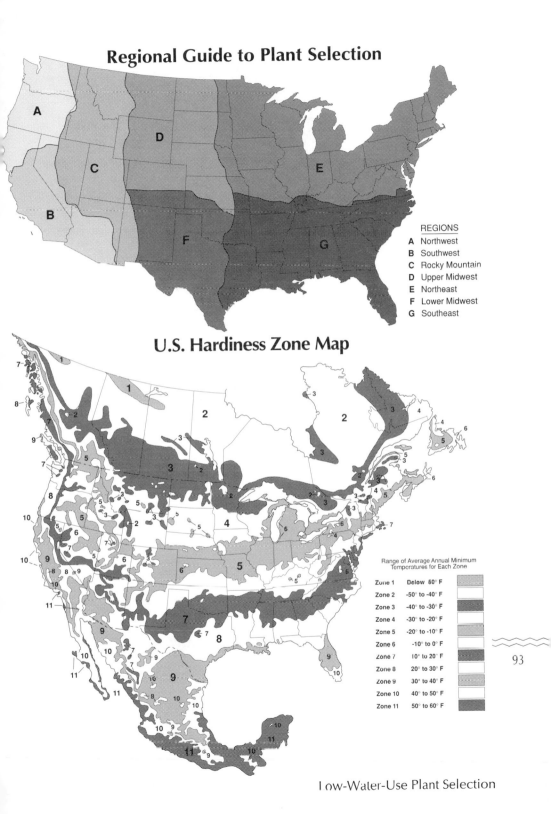

REGIONS
A Northwest
B Southwest
C Rocky Mountain
D Upper Midwest
E Northeast
F Lower Midwest
G Southeast

U.S. Hardiness Zone Map

Range of Average Annual Minimum
Temperatures for Each Zone

Zone 1	Below -50° F
Zone 2	-50° to -40° F
Zone 3	-40° to -30° F
Zone 4	-30° to -20° F
Zone 5	-20° to -10° F
Zone 6	-10° to 0° F
Zone 7	10° to 20° F
Zone 8	20° to 30° F
Zone 9	30° to 40° F
Zone 10	40° to 50° F
Zone 11	50° to 60° F

93

Low-Water-Use Plant Selection

Low-Water-Use Plant Selections

NOTE: After the description of each of the following plants, there is a letter(s) and a number(s). The letter specifies the region(s) where the plant may be grown successfully and the number(s) indicates the hardiness zone (range) of the plant. Use the Regional Guide to Plant Selection on page 93 to determine your region and to guide you in your plant selection; use the Hardiness Zone Map on page 93 to check the hardiness of your selected plant. The designations on both maps are *general* guidelines. Also, consult the Plant Selection Guide on pages 119 to 130 for a quick reference. Ask your local nursery owner for more detailed information about selected plants for use in your area.

Trees and Shrubs for Color, Ornament, Screens & Windbreaks

Acacia *(Acacia spp.)* are evergreen trees or shrubs that are hardy, tough, and drought resistant. B F G, 9 to 10 Sydney golden wattle *(A. longifolia)* is used frequently as dust and headlight screens along highways in California and Arizona. B G, 9 to 10 The kangaroo thorn *(A. armata)* is a barrier shrub with formidable thorns to keep out people and animals. B, 9 to 10 There are hundreds of species with cascades of yellow, golden, or orange blooms, but only about twenty species in common use. They will grow to 20 feet in about 3 years, but live only 20 to 30 years. They grow in mild winter climates only, but will survive high desert winter frosts quite well.

Australian-pine *(Casuarina spp.)* (also known as beefwood or she-oak) are not true pines even though they have needles. *C. cunninghamiana* grows to 70 feet. It is a good tree for tough soil conditions. Its impressive silhouette makes it ideal as a background or handsome single focus tree. There also are fast growing hybrids of this tree. B F G, 10

Australian-willow *(Geijera parviflora)* is an evergreen tree that reaches about 30 feet high and 20 feet wide. It is a fine-textured, graceful tree with main branches that grow up and out, while small branches and leaves droop down giving a willow effect. It is excellent in a grove, on a patio, or as a single focus tree. It is very drought resistant, but not good in clay soil. B F G, 9 to 10

94

Bottletree *(Brachychiton populneus)* (also known as *Sterculia diversifolia)* is a pyramid shaped evergreen tree that grows to 30 or 50 feet high. It has whitish, bell shaped flowers and shiny foliage. It is useful as a single focus tree or in rows as a screen or windbreak. B, 9 to 10

California black walnut *(Juglans hindsii)* is a broad-crowned deciduous tree that grows to 30 to 60 feet high and has edible nuts. It is ideal as a single focus tree. Do not plant it near a patio or parking area because it is aphid-prone and drips sticky honeydew all summer. It is very drought resistant. A B, 8 to 10

California buckeye *(Aesculus californica)* is a small, shrublike horse chestnut tree that grows to 10 to 20 feet high and has rich green foliage with creamy flowers. Since it is very wide spreading, it needs room to grow. A B, 8 to 10

Carob *(Ceratonia siliqua)* (also known as St.-John's-bread) is an evergreen tree or shrub. Lower branches must be pruned to make a 30 to 40 foot tree with a dense, round head. It has dark green foliage and large, leathery, edible seed pods. It is very drought resistant. Because the roots need lots of room to spread and grow, do not plant it near the street — the roots may heave up paving stones. B, 10

Cedar *(Cedrus* spp.) are evergreen trees and all species are deep-rooted and drought resistant. *C. deodara* is a fast growing, large tree (80 feet high, 40 feet wide) with graceful, upswept branches. A cedar tree can be pruned to grow as a low or high spreading shrub or can be a picturesque single focus tree. A to G, 6 to 9

Chinaberry *(Melia azedarach)* is a deciduous tree with lilac flowers and grows to 30 to 50 feet high. It is very picturesque with hard, yellow fruit that is poisonous in quantity, but birds enjoy it. B F, 9 to 10

Cypress *(Cupressus* spp.) are coniferous evergreen trees that make good hedges, screens, or stand-alone highlights. Tecate cypress *(C. forbesii)* is a fast growing, low branching tree that grows to 20 feet high and is ideal for a hedge or screen. B G, 9 to 10 Smooth-barked Arizona cypress *(C. glabra)* is valued in the desert as a fast growing windbreak tree or tall screen; it is very drought resistant and grows to 40 feet high with a 20-foot spread. A B G, 8 to 10 Monterey cypress *(C. macrocarpa)* should be grown in coastal regions only. It is a very picturesque tree that grows to 40 feet high and is an effective windbreak. B G, 8 to 10 Italian cypress *(C. sempervirens)* is commonly sold as a graceful, dense, columnlike tree that grows to 60 feet high. A B G, 8 to 10

Elm *(Ulmus* spp.*)* are deciduous or partially evergreen trees. The genus, however, is often associated with wet soils. The Siberian elm *(U. pumila),* though, grows to 50 feet high and is relatively drought tolerant. It tolerates poor soil conditions and makes a good windbreak. Large roots, however, make this tree troublesome in a garden setting. A to F, 4 to 9

Eucalyptus *(Eucalyptus* spp.*)* are evergreen trees or shrubs. They are very popular in California and Arizona for windbreaks, for firewood, and for beauty. Most eucalyptus are quite drought tolerant. *E. preissiana* has magnificent, yellow flowers with shrublike growth from 8 to 12 feet high; silver princess *(E. caesia)* has masses of rose pink flowers and grows to 15 to 20 feet high; *E. macrocarpa* has vivid crimson flowers and grows to 15 to 25 feet high. The lemon-scented gum *(E. citriodora)* is a magnificent and graceful tree that soars to 75 to 100 feet. It is dramatic as a single focus tree and can grow close to patios, walkways, and walls without problems. B F G, 9 to 10

Fig *(Ficus* spp.*)* are deciduous trees with many species. All are picturesque and make fine ornamental trees. They grow rapidly to 15 to 30 feet, but hard freezing will reduce them to shrubs. B F G, 10

Floss-silk tree *(Chorisia speciosa)* is an evergreen tree that becomes deciduous when temperatures drop below freezing. It is a wonderful highlight tree in the garden and grows to 50 or 60 feet high with a stout, green trunk that is studded with spines. It has attractive pink or white blooms. B G, 9 to 10

Golden raintree *(Koelreuteria paniculata)* is a deciduous tree and has clusters of small, yellow flowers and papery fruit capsules that look like lanterns. It grows to 35 feet high and makes a good patio tree. This is an excellent tree in alkaline soil and high wind or drought conditions. It also is suitable for the lawn or at street side. A B F G, 5 to 9

Grevillea *(Grevillea* spp.*)* are evergreen trees or shrubs that grow to 100 feet high and have long, slender flowers with fine-textured foliage. They thrive in high heat and drought conditions and are excellent shade trees. All species are very drought resistant. B G, 10

Hackberry *(Celtis spp.)* are deciduous trees that are similar to elm, but smaller (8 to 120 feet high). Most species are quite drought resistant and excellent in high heat and windy desert areas. They are good shade or street trees that can be located close to driveways and buildings without problems. Common hackberry *(C. occidentalis)* is native to the eastern United States and grows to 120 feet high. A to G, 4 to 9

Ironwood *(Lyonothamnus floribundus asplenifolius)* (also known as Catalina ironwood) is an evergreen tree with redwood-colored bark and very distinctive leaves — glossy, deep green above and gray and hairy underneath. It is a handsome grove tree that grows to 30 to 60 feet high. B G, 10

Jacaranda *(Jacaranda mimosifolia)* is a deciduous or evergreen tree with fernlike leaves and clusters of lavender flowers. It is excellent as a street tree or as a large patio tree and grows to 25 to 40 feet high, 15 to 30 feet wide. It is very drought resistant. B F G, 10

Jerusalem thorn *(Parkinsonia aculeata)* (also known as Mexican palo verde tree) is a deciduous tree and very picturesque with yellow-green bark, spiny twigs, and clusters of yellow flowers. It grows to 15 to 30 feet high and is very tolerant of alkaline soils and drought. With its spare foliage, which filters rather than shades the sun, and its thorns, this tree would not blend well in a tailored garden, but will look perfect in a water-conserving landscape. B F G, 9 to 10

Jujube *(Ziziphus jujuba)* (also known as Chinese jujube) is a deciduous tree with glossy, green leaves and small, yellowish flowers; its leaves turn yellow in the fall. Jujube is a good decorative tree that grows to 20 to 30 feet high. It grows very well in saline or alkaline soil and is quite drought resistant. B, 8 to 10

Kentucky coffee tree *(Gymnocladus dioica)* is an upright, very distinctive looking deciduous tree that grows to 50 feet high. It has fine-textured foliage and distinctive, bare branches in the winter; it is a good tree for adding form to the garden. It withstands cold winters and poor soil conditions, but is less drought tolerant than most of the trees that are listed here. A B E G, 5 to 9

Linden *(Tilia spp.)* are deciduous trees with dense, compact crowns and clusters of fragrant, yellow-white flowers. Silver linden *(T.*

tomentosa) reaches 40 to 50 feet high and is the only linden that can be classified as drought resistant. Other species require regular watering. A B C E F G, 5 to 9

Locust *(Robinia* spp.*)* are deciduous, fast growing, and hardy trees and shrubs with clusters of pink or white blooms. 'Idahoensis' *(R. x ambigua)* is perhaps the showiest locust for a garden or patio. *R. neomexicana* is a shrub that grows to 6 feet high and is very drought resistant. A to G, 4 to 9

Loquat *(Eriobotrya japonica)* is an evergreen tree that grows to 15 to 30 feet high and produces a tasty fruit. It is a good lawn tree that does well in sunshine or shade. A B F G, 8 to 10

Mexican blue palm *(Brahea armata)* is an ornamental tree that performs very well under drought conditions, but is hardy only to 18°F. It has silvery blue leaves with creamy flowers and grows to 40 to 60 feet high. It is especially sturdy under high heat and high wind conditions. B F G, 9 to 10

Oak *(Quercus* spp.*)* can be both evergreen or deciduous trees (two different species). Both species are vigorous growers, but will dominate a garden with their deep root systems. An oak is an excellent shade or focal point tree and some species can grow to 100 feet high. Of the dozens of oak species, most of the native western and western Mediterranean species are drought tolerant. A B D E F G, 4 to 9

Olive *(Olea europaea)* is a willowy evergreen tree with soft, gray-green foliage that grows to 25 feet high. It thrives in hot, dry summers and is hardy to 15°F. Olives dropping from the tree in the fall can damage other plants, especially lawn grass, if left on the ground; they also will stain driveways. Trim fruiting branches early or shake down ripe fruit and dispose. This tree performs well as a windscreen or as a decorative highlight in a garden. B F G, 8 to 10

Osage-orange *(Maclura pomifera)* is a fast growing deciduous tree with very thorny branches. It will grow to 60 feet high and can be pruned to be a rough hedge or background screen. It survives poor soil, high heat, drought, and cold. A B D E F G, 5 to 9

98

Palms are some of the most varied and widely used plants, either as lofty accent trees along avenues or in smaller genera as shrublike palms in gardens. Palms are excellent around swimming pools because they do not drop leaves into the water. Many palms, such as *Brahea* spp. (to 40 feet), *Chamaerops* spp. (to 20 feet), *Phoenix* spp. (to 100 feet), and *Washingtonia* spp. (to 100 feet), need no irrigation once they are established. B F G, 9 to 10

Palo verde *(Cercidium floridum)* is a deciduous desert tree that grows to 10 to 30 feet high and adds beauty to many desert gardens. It has bright yellow flowers that almost hide the tree; its small seed pods are a favorite with birds. It survives drought, high heat, winds, and severe frost, but is not a tree for long, very cold winter regions. B, 9 to 10

Pepper tree *(Schinus* spp.*)* are evergreen or deciduous trees that are drought tolerant and make good shade or single focus trees with magnificently gnarled and convoluted branches. Two varieties are especially popular. First, the California pepper tree *(S. molle)* is an evergreen and grows very fast to 25 to 40 feet high. It grows in almost any soil, but has a very aggressive surface root system, so do not plant near sidewalks, patios, sewers, or driveways. It is best for informal spaces, possibly as a shade tree in a play area. Its fruit attracts birds, but there is a lot of tree litter, particularly the small, red berries that leave stains if not cleaned up. Second, the Brazilian pepper *(S. terebinthifolius)* is a good shade or patio tree if you train it well and do not encourage vigorous surface root growth with fertilizer and frequent watering. Peppers are distinctive and beautiful trees that thrive in lower altitude desert areas in Arizona and California, but will not tolerate sustained cold or frost. Both these species could become pests if grown in the Southwest or Southeast, so be aware and control their growth. B F G, 9 to 10

Pine *(Pinus* spp.*)* is an evergreen family of trees with a great variety of foliage and sizes (30 to 90 feet). Pine trees will grow in almost any type of soil or climate. One of the most drought resistant is Italian stone pine *(P. pinea)*. B F G, 8 to 10 For alkaline soils, try Japanese black pine *(P. thunbergiana)*, which is a small rounded tree that grows to 20 feet in the desert and to 100 feet in the Northwest; it is also popular as a bonsai tree or container plant. A to G, 5 to 9 *P. ponderosa* grows to 200 feet and is native throughout western North America. It is used primarily for timber, but also can be used as a good background tree. A B C, 5 to 9 Most pines can be used as screens or windbreaks, but many are fine stand-alone or background trees; all can be shaped as they grow.

Pistache *(Pistacia* spp.*)* are ornamental deciduous trees that grow to 60 feet high and 50 feet wide. Pistaches make good ornamental trees and need infrequent but deep watering. Only *P. vera* bears edible nuts; it also withstands considerable drought. Chinese pistache *(P. chinenis)* boasts brilliant scarlet, orange, and crimson foliage in the fall. It is an ideal patio or street side tree. B F G, 9 to 10

Redbud *(Cercis* spp.*)* are deciduous trees or shrubs with attractive heart shaped leaves and clusters of flowers. Only the western redbud *(C. occidentalis)*, which grows to 8 to 18 feet high, is drought resistant. It has blue-green leaves, red bean pods, and red flowers. It is excellent for defining garden areas. A B E F G, 7 to 9

Silk tree *(Albizia julibrissin)* is a deciduous tree that grows to 40 feet high with leaves that fold up at night and pink, puffy flowers. It is drought tolerant and flourishes in the hot sun. Its flat top makes it a good shade tree for patio areas. B F G, 5 to 10

Sumac *(Rhus* spp.*)* are evergreen or deciduous trees or shrubs and are extremely hardy, even in poor soils. There are a number of evergreen and deciduous sumac trees and shrubs that will grow under difficult conditions, but the evergreens need good drainage. The deciduous species are a bit hardier than evergreens. African sumac *(R. lancea)* is a slow growing evergreen that grows to 25 feet with graceful, weeping branchlets that are similar to a willow. It endures very high heat and is drought resistant. It is a good tree for screens, hedges, and erosion control on slopes. B F G, 8 to 10

Tamarisk *(Tamarix* spp.*)* are deciduous or evergreen-appearing trees or shrubs that grow well in the difficult conditions of high wind, drought, or very saline soils. The athel *(T. aphylla)* is a favorite windbreak tree in desert areas with fast growth to 10 feet or more in 3 years and to 30 to 50 feet over 15 years. Roots will grow hundreds of feet, horizontal or vertical, to find water, so do not plant near the house or swimming pool. This species may become weedy in western regions of the country. B F G, 9 to 10

Tristania *(Tristania* spp.*)* are evergreen trees that are related to the eucalyptus. They are extremely handsome trees that grow from 30 to 60 feet high with reddish brown, peeling bark and handsome foliage. Grown in warm climates only, they are very drought resistant and are good street or lawn trees. B F G, 9 to 10

Umbrella tree *(Melia azedarach* cv. 'Umbraculiformis'*)* is a Texas favorite that has a dense, dome-shaped crown that grows to 30 feet high and provides very dense shade. It is extremely hardy in poor soil and drought conditions. A B F G, 9 to 10

SHRUBS FOR FOLIAGE & FLOWERS

Apache-plume *(Fallugia paradoxa)* is a partially evergreen shrub that is found throughout California, Nevada, Texas, Utah, Arizona, Colorado, and Texas and can be grown as far north as Massachusetts. It grows to 3 to 8 feet high and has small, deep green leaves and flowers that look like white roses. It is very drought tolerant and useful for erosion control. B F, 6 to 9

Artemisia *(Artemisia* spp.*)* cover a range of evergreen or deciduous shrubs and woody perennials with aromatic foliage and silvery gray or white leaves; they are more familiar as wormwood, sagebrush, and tarragon. All are drought resistant and good for background use with brighter perennials. A to G, 4 to 10 Common sagebrush *(A. tridentata)* is a rounded evergreen shrub with very aromatic, silver-gray foliage that grows to 10 feet high. A B C F, 4 to 10 Sand sage *(A. filifolia)* is a wide branching shrub that grows to 5 feet high. B C D F, 5 to 10 Silver sage *(A. cana)* is also wide branching, but only grows to 3 feet high. A B C, 4 to 10

Bottlebrush *(Callistemon* spp.*)* are evergreen shrubs for mild areas only (at 20°F or below, they are severely damaged). They are fast growing with spikes of red or yellow flowers and are very drought tolerant; some species can be trained into trees. Bottlebrush can be trained as wall covers, screens, and windbreaks. The most tolerant of heat and cold is *C. citrinus,* which grows to 25 feet high and is a favorite of hummingbirds. B F G, 9 to 10

California holly grape *(Mahonia pinnata)* (also known as *Berberis pinnata*) is one of many species of evergreen shrubs with dense, spikelike clusters of yellow flowers and blackish berries that attract birds. All species are drought tolerant, but need some shade in desert areas. *M. pinnata* grows to about 6 feet high. It can be used as a screen or placed among trees. A B F G, 7 to 10

101

Cape plumbago *(Plumbago auriculata)* (also known as leadwort) is a semievergreen shrub that grows to 6 feet tall and 8 to 10 feet wide.

It is a good background shrub or cover for a fence or bank. It has light to medium green leaves with white to very light blue clusters of flowers. Heavy frost damages them, but they will recover. B F G, 9 to 10

Cotoneaster *(Cotoneaster* spp.*)* are evergreen or deciduous shrubs in a wide range of species and forms, from ground covers to small and large upright shrubs (to 20 feet). They grow well in poor soils. They have graceful, arching branches that give them a fountainlike shape with white or pinkish blossoms and colorful winter berries. They are very versatile drought-resistant plants for use as background, screens, or hedges and are adaptable to hot or cold climates. A to G, 5 to 9

Coyote brush *(Baccharis pilularis)* (also known as chaparral broom) is an extremely adaptable evergreen shrub that has a dense, billowing mat of bright green foliage and grows to 5 feet high. It is excellent for bank covers or other difficult site conditions. It is very drought resistant, but is not a cold climate plant. B F G, 6 to 9

Crape-myrtle *(Lagerstroemia indica)* is a deciduous shrub with many cultivars that have various colored flower clusters. It can be trained as a shrub tree (6 to 30 feet high) with smooth, pink bark. It is drought resistant, but not successful in colder climes. B F G, 7 to 10

Elaeagnus *(Elaeagnus* spp.*)* are deciduous and evergreen large shrubs or small trees. All species grow rapidly and become dense, firm, tough shrubs that grow from 6 to 15 feet high. They make effective barrier plants, clipped hedges, and windscreens. The evergreens have a silvery sparkle on the leaves and are fairly drought resistant. Silverberry *(E. commutata),* a deciduous shrub, is native to Canada and the northern plains and is a good choice for cold climates. A to G, 3 to 9

Euonymus *(Euonymus* spp.*)* are evergreen or deciduous shrubs and evergreen vines. With their striking foliage, texture, and form, they are favorites with landscape designers to add structure to a garden. Their colorful fruit attracts many birds. *E. fortunei* is a fine evergreen trailing vine that can grow to 40 feet long with rich, dark green leaves. Euonymus are some of the best performing evergreens where temperatures drop below 0°F. A to G, 4 to 9

Flannelbush *(Fremontodendron californicum)* is a fast growing evergreen shrub with leathery, dark green leaves, which are covered in feltlike hairs underneath, and yellow, saucerlike flowers. It is excellent for hillside plantings or as a backdrop for other plants. It is very drought resistant and grows to 15 feet high. B C F, 9 to 10

Germander *(Teucrium spp.)* is a hardy family of evergreen shrubs and subshrubs and can grow up to 6 feet in some species. They are drought tolerant and will grow in rocky or poor soils. The reddish, purplish plants make an attractive backdrop for more colorful plants, or they can be grown as an informal hedge or screen. A B E F G, 7 to 10

Grevillea *(Grevillea thelamanniana)* is an evergreen shrub that is fine textured and showy and grows to 5 feet high. It is a good plant for poor, rocky soils, but cannot tolerate more than occasional dips in temperatures below freezing. There are more than a dozen species available of varying sizes and blooms (pink, red, crimson, yellow). They all are very drought resistant. B F G, 10

Hopbush *(Dodonaea cuneata)* is a warm climate shrub that is native to Arizona. Upright stems grow fast to 12 to 15 feet high and almost as wide with willowy, green leaves. It is a good plant for a trimmed hedge or informal screen. It is quite drought resistant, but will survive among plants that require regular watering. It also will grow in any kind of soil, in dry deserts, and along ocean coasts. B F G, 8 to 10

Juniper *(Juniperus spp.)* are evergreen shrubs growing to several heights with needlelike foliage in many shades of green. Many species will survive desert heat and mountain frosts. They are extremely versatile and hardy shrubs for use as accents, low screen hedges, and in some species, for use horizontally as ground covers (see page 115). A to G, 3 to 10

Lavender *(Lavandula spp.)* are very fragrant evergreen shrubs and herbs for use as edgings, low hedges, or singly in a spice garden. They are favorites in many water-conserving gardens. A B E F G, 7 to 9

Leadplant *(Amorpha canescens)* (also known as false indigo) is a deciduous shrub that grows to 4 feet high. It has small, dark blue or purple flowers and fernlike foliage of white hairy leaflets. It tolerates dry soil extremely well. A B D E F G, 3 to 7

103

Manzanita *(Arctostaphylos* spp.*)* are widely grown western evergreen shrubs that grow from low spreading to 5- to 6-feet-high shrubs with gray-green foliage. They have distinctive, crooked branches and red-purple bark; their fruit attracts birds. They are good plants for steep banks, but they do not do well in the shade. A B, 7 to 10

Mountain-mahogany *(Cercocarpus* spp.*)* are tall evergreen or decid-uous shrubs that are found throughout the West and can grow to 25 feet high. They can be used as shrubs or hedges. *C. montanus* is an exceptional shrub in cold, dry, sunny mountain regions. A B C D F, 4 to 9

Mesquite *(Prosopis glandulosa torreyana)* is a deciduous shrub or tree with large, deep roots and grows to 25 feet high. It is native to southwestern deserts. It has tiny, bright green leaflets and is a good windscreen or windbreak. B C F, 5 to 9

Myrtle *(Myrtus* spp.*)* are drought-resistant evergreen shrubs that can be grown outdoors only in hotter climates. They grow to 15 feet high. They make excellent informal hedges or screens or can stand alone as large shrubs with white, sweet-scented flowers. B F G, 8 to 10

Nanking cherry *(Prunus tomentosa)* is a very hardy deciduous shrub. It has white blossoms and grows to 6 or 8 feet high. It is similar to western sand cherry *(P. besseyi),* which is a deciduous shrub that grows 3 to 6 feet high with delicious black fruit. Of the many flowering cherries, these two species will survive cold, heat, wind, and drought. A to G, 3 to 9

Oleander *(Nerium oleander)* is an evergreen shrub that produces flowers and greenery throughout desert regions and grows to 20 feet high. Its colored flowers vary from white, salmon, pink, and yellow. It thrives in heat, poor soil, and drought conditions. The stems and leaves of the oleander are poisonous for animals and humans. Use as a screen, windbreak, or garden border. If deer are a problem in your area, they will not touch oleander. B F G, 9 to 10

Photinia *(Photinia serrulata)* is an evergreen shrub that is related to the hawthorn with very attractive, long, deep green leaves and white flowers and red berries. It will grow to 35 feet if not trimmed, but is best as a dense shrub, 10 feet by 10 feet. It is reasonably drought resistant once established and will freeze in continued 0° to 10°F temperatures, but will recover. B F G, 7 to 10

Piñon Pine *(Pinus edulis)* is a slow growing (10 to 20 feet), bushy evergreen tree that can function as a distinctive shrub. It is excellent for new gardens, containers, or rock gardens. It also is drought resistant, and the nuts are edible. A B C D F, 4 to 9

Poinciana *(Caesalpinia gilliesii)* (also known as bird-of-paradise bush) is a deciduous or evergreen shrub with clusters of yellow blooms with long, bright red stamens. It is a showy bush for mild climes and will drop leaves in a cold winter. It also freezes to the ground in colder areas, but can be cutback in the fall and will rebound in the spring. It is a fast growing but straggly plant and is very useful for a quick screen, but it needs twice monthly watering for the best blooms. B G, 10

Pomegranate *(Punica granatum)* is a deciduous shrub or tree that grows to 20 feet high or more with glossy, bright green leaves and orange-red flowers and fruit. It is good for desert areas and poor soils — even heavy alkaline soils. Its fruit is a bonus for you or the birds. It makes a good, dense, low hedge and will survive high desert frost, but check hardiness before planting. B G, 9 to 10

Rockrose *(Cistus spp.)* are sun-loving evergreen shrubs that grow to 2 to 6 feet high and are covered with white or pink blooms; it is hardy only to 15°F. A variety of species and cultivars make these shrubs versatile, beautiful plants for use as hedges, dividers, informal screens, bank covers, or for interplanting with other drought-resistant plants. A B F G, 7 to 10

Rose *(Rosa rugosa)* (also known as Turkestan rose) is a deciduous shrub and grows to 3 to 8 feet high with 3- to 4-inch flowers that are white and creamy yellow to purplish red. It makes an excellent hedge or accent shrub. It is very hardy and can endure hard freezes, wind, and salt spray, but is less drought tolerant than the following species. Austrian copper rose *(R. foetida)* grows to 10 feet high and has 2-inch yellow flowers; red-leaved rose *(R. rubrifolia)* grows to 6 to 7 feet high with 1H-inch reddish pink flowers; and woods rose *(R. woodsii)* has 1I-inch pink or white flowers and grows to 6 feet high. All are very drought resistant. A to G, 2 to 9

Rosemary *(Rosmarinus officinalis)* is an aromatic evergreen shrub that can grow to 2 to 6 feet high and has light blue flowers. It tolerates hot sun and poor soil. Taller shrubs make good clipped hedges or borders. Low growing varieties are good for ground or bank covers. A to G, 7 to 10

Sage *(Salvia leucantha)* (also known as Mexican bush sage) is the deciduous shrub form of sage. It grows to 2 to 4 feet high and 2 to 4 feet wide and has very attractive, tubular, purple or deep rose spikes with white flowers. It is frost sensitive, but drought tolerant. Autumn sage *(S. greggii)* grows to 3 feet high and has beautiful purple-red flowers. It is very drought resistant. There are many species of drought-tolerant sages, but many are very flammable. Be aware of this if you live in fire-prone areas. B F G, 9 to 10

Saltbush *(Atriplex spp.)* are evergreen or deciduous shrubs that are valued for their gray or silvery foliage. They are very drought tolerant and are good plants for fire and erosion control. Some species can be trimmed as hedges. Four-wing saltbush *(A. canescens)* grows to 6 feet high and has gray-winged leaves. Quailbush *(A. lentiformus)* has silvery gray foliage and grows to 6 to 10 feet high. Both of these species are excellent plants for erosion control and large drought-tolerant gardens or landscapes. A B C D F, 4 to 10

Silk-tassel bush *(Garrya spp.)* are evergreen shrubs that are native in coastal ranges from Oregon to California. *G. fremontii* tolerates drought and cold well. It has yellow-green leaves and yellow or purplish catkins and grows to 15 feet high. It makes a very decorative shrub or screen. A B F G, 8 to 10

Xylosma *(Xylosma congestum)* is an evergreen or deciduous shrub or small tree. It is a very handsome and versatile plant that grows to 8 to 10 feet high with oval, yellowish green leaves. It is adaptable to most soils, heat tolerant, and drought resistant. Plants are hardy to 10°F, but will lose many leaves in sharp frost. Use as a shrub, ground or bank cover, clipped or unclipped hedge, or as espalier on a wall or fence. A B F G, 8 to 10

Yucca *(Yucca spp.)* are evergreen shrubs with some species growing to 25 feet high. They have cup shaped, white flowers with a rose or purple tinge. They are very drought tolerant and do well in well-drained sandy soils, but species vary in hardiness so check with your nursery owner. Spanish bayonet *(Y. aloifolia)* grows to 25 feet high B C F, 6 to 9; datil *(Y. baccata)* grows to 18 feet high. B C F, 5 to 9

Soapweed *(Y. glauca)* has a short, woody trunk and grows to only 8 feet high   C D F, 4 to 9; soaptree *(Y. elata)* is also shorter with a 12-foot growth. B C F, 6 to 10 Our-Lord's-candle *(Y. whipplei)* grows to 12 feet high and is by far the most striking species when in bloom. B, 9 to 10

PERENNIALS & ANNUALS FOR COLOR
& LOW MAINTENANCE

Agave *(Agave* spp.*)* are perennial succulents with long, fleshy leaves. There are small and large species that grow to 5 feet across. They are warm climate plants and cannot tolerate frost. B F G, 7 to 10

Aloe *(Aloe arborescens)* is a showy perennial succulent that is a member of the lily family. It has fleshy, pointed leaves with orange, yellow, cream, and red flowers. It survives light frost. A G, 10

Anacyclus *(Anacyclus depressus)* is a hardy perennial with a dense mat of grayish leaves and daisylike, white flowers with red reverses. It will need some winter protection if grown in cold climates. A B C F, 6 to 9

Belladonna *(Amaryllis belladonna)* is a perennial bulb that is a good plant in mild winter areas. It has clusters of pink, trumpet shaped flowers and grows in any soil. A B F G, 5 to 10

Blue-eyed-grass *(Sisyrinchium bellum)* is a California native perennial. It is tall with greenish blue leaves and purple flowers. B G, 9 to 10

Buckwheat *(Eriogonum* spp.*)* are herbaceous annuals, perennials, or ground covers that are native to the West. They can withstand heat, wind, and drought and grow well among rocks or massed on banks. They have clouds of pale yellow, white, pink, or red flowers. A B C D F G, 4 to 10

Capeweed *(Arctotheca calendula)* is an evergreen perennial and a rapid spreading ground cover with big yellow, daisy flowers. It can survive mild frosts. A B F G, 8

Coreopsis *(Coreopsis* spp.*)* are annuals or perennials of the Aster Family with radiantly colorful flowers in yellow, orange, or magenta that bloom throughout the summer. They are excellent plants in borders or as edging for defined areas; *C. lanceolata* and *C. tinctoria* are especially suited for those uses. A to G, 5 to 9

Cosmos *(Cosmos* spp.*)* are very showy annuals with white, pink, or magenta daisylike flowers. They produce great color in borders or as background and attract birds to the garden. A to G, 5 to 9

Dudleya *(Dudleya* spp.*)* are rosette-forming perennial succulents with fleshy leaves that are covered with chalky powder. They are very striking plants, but need protection from rain, hail, and frost. They are also good container plants. B G, 10

Echeveria *(Echeveria* spp.*)* are perennials with fleshy-leaved, gray or green rosettes and bell shaped yellow, red, or pink flowers. They are very attractive plants and grow well in containers. B G, 10

Euryops *(Euryops* spp.*)* are evergreen perennials with daisylike flowers. They are fast growing and long blooming. *E. acraeus* is the most hardy during a frost. B G, 9 to 10

Evening-primrose *(Oenothera* spp.*)* (See page 114.)

Flax *(Linum* spp.*)* are annuals and perennials. They are long blooming with blue, white, or yellow flowers and are excellent plants in borders. *L. perenne,* with its variety *L. lewisii,* is the hardiest species. A to G, 4 to 10

Gaillardia *(Gaillardia* spp.*)* are annuals and perennials from the central and western United States. They have daisylike flowers in yellow, bronze, and scarlet. They are excellent for borders and cut flowers. *G. pulchella* is a popular annual with large yellow flowers; *G. aristata* is a long blooming perennial. A to G, 4 to 9

Gay-feather *(Liatris* spp.*)* are perennials that are native to the central and eastern United States. Tufts of narrow, grassy leaves extend to tall, narrow stems that are topped by rosy purple, fluffy flower heads. They are good plants in mixed borders and can survive heat, cold, drought, and poor soil. D E F G, 4 to 9

Horehound *(Marrubium vulgare)* is a perennial herb with wrinkled, aromatic, gray-green leaves and white flowers. Use for edging. A to G, 4 to 9

Indigo *(Baptisia australis)* is a perennial that is native to the eastern United States. It grows from 3 to 6 feet high with blue-green leaves and indigo blue blooms that are shaped like a sweet pea blossom. E G, 5 to 9

Iceplant *(Mesembryanthemum* spp.*)* are perennial succulents for warm climates. They have pale yellow or rose-colored flowers and are very resistant to disease, insects, and smog. Use for bank coverings, sandy areas, and erosion control. B G, 9 to 10

Iris *(Iris* spp.*)* are perennial bulbs or rhizomes with a multitude of species and flower color. Bearded irises *(Pogon)* are more drought resistant than other species. Be sure to check the drought resistance of any iris species you choose; many iris species grow well only in wet or moist soils. A to G, 2 to 9

Jerusalem-sage *(Phlomis fruticosa)* is a shrubby perennial with woolly, gray-green leaves and yellow flowers. It does well in poor soil and is good for dry slopes and mixed borders. B F G, 7

Lion's-ear *(Leonotis leonuris)* is a shrubby perennial with deep orange flowers. It is very striking and thrives in full sun. B G, 10

Matilija poppy *(Romneya coulteri)* is a perennial that is native to southern California. It is a wonderful display plant that grows to 8 feet high with 9-inch-wide, white, papery petals. Use on hillsides or in wide borders because the roots are very invasive. A B, 9 to 10

Mexican-sunflower *(Tithonia rotundifolia)* is a perennial that is used in northern, colder regions as a tender annual. It is a rapid grower and can grow to 12 feet with colorful 3-inch-wide flowers with orange-scarlet rays and tufted, yellow centers. It is a good plant for desert gardens and as a background plant. A to G, 5 to 9

New-Zealand-flax *(Phormium tenax)* is an evergreen perennial with swordlike, vertical leaves. It is very dramatic as a focal point plant and is sturdy and fast growing in almost any soil. B F G, 9 to 10

Puya *(Puya berteroniana)* is an evergreen perennial for warm climates. It is a large spectacular plant with massive, metallic, blue-green and turquoise flowers. Use for banks, rock gardens, and containers. B G, 9 to 10

Red valerian *(Centranthus ruber)* is a bushy perennial that grows to 3 feet high with bluish green leaves and small, crimson or pink flowers. It is a good plant for banks, walls, or rough areas and is a prolific self-sower. A to G, 5 to 9

109

Rose-moss *(Portulaca grandiflora)* is an annual with brilliant red, pink, orange, yellow, white, and cerise, roselike flowers. Plant in rock

MORE COLOR FOR A
WATER-CONSERVING GARDEN

*If you love English-style gardens, choose from these plants
for a lavish English perennial or mixed border.*

Botanical Name	Common Name
Achillea millefolium cvs.	Common yarrow
Agapanthus africanus	African-lily
Alcea rosea	Hollyhock
Alyogyne huegeli	Blue hibiscus
Anigozanthus spp.	Kangaroo-paw
Armeria maritima	Thrift
Artemesia schmidtiana 'Nana'	Silvermound
Aurinia saxatilis	Basket-of-gold
Capparis spinosa	Caper bush
Carissa grandiflora	Natal plum
Cassia artemisioides	Wormwood
Cerastium tomentosum	Snow-in-summer
Chamelaucium uncinatum	Geraldton wax plant
Cheiranthus cheiri cvs.	Wallflower
Chrysanthemum frutescens cvs.	Marguerite daisy
Cistus ladanifer	Laudanum
Convolvulus tricolor	Dwarf morning-glory
Coreopsis auriculata 'Nana'	Coreopsis
Coreopsis verticillata cvs.	Coreopsis
Correa pulchella	Correa
Cotula spp.	Cotula
Dianthus plumarius	Pinks
Dicliptera suberecta	Dicliptera
Diosma ericoides	Breath-of-heaven
Echium fastuosum	Viper's bugloss
Euryops pectinatus	Gray-leaved euryops
Eurypops pectinatus 'Viridis'	Green-leaved euryops
Gaillardia grandiflora cvs.	Blanketflower
Gaillardia pulchella cvs.	Blanketflower
Gaura lindheimeri	Gaura
Gazania rigens leucolaena	Treasureflower
Gypsophila repens	Baby's-breath
Helianthemum nummularium	Sun-rose
Helichrysum angustifolium	White-leaf everlasting
Helichrysum petiolatum	Licorice plant
Justicia spicigera	Water willow

Justicia rizzinii	Water willow
Kniphofia uvaria cvs.	Red-hot-poker
Lantana spp.	Verbena shrub
Lavandula angustifolia	English lavender
Lavandula dentata	French lavender
Lavandula latifolia	Spike lavender
Lavandula stoechas	Spanish lavender
Lavatera assurgentiflora	Mallow
Limonium perezii	Statice
Linum flavum	Golden flax
Lobelia laxiflora	Mexican lobelia
Mahonia nervosa	Oregon-grape
Mahonia repens	Creeping mahonia
Nandina domestica cvs.	Heavenly-bamboo
Narcissus triandrus	Daffodil
Nierembergia hippomanica violacea	Dwarf cupflower
Pelargonium x hortorum	Common Geranium
Pelargonium peltatum	Ivy Geranium
Penstemon eatonii	Beardtongue
Perovskia atriplicifolia	Russian sage
Punica granatum 'Nana'	Dwarf pomegranate
Ribes aureum	Golden currant
Ribes sanguineum	Red flowering currant
Ruscus aculeatus	Butcher's-broom
Salvia argentea	Silver sage
Salvia officinalis cvs.	Common sage
Salvia clevelandii	Blue sage
Santolina chamaecyparissus	Lavender-cotton
Santolina rosmarinifolia	Lavender shrub
Sedum cvs. *"Rosy Glow"*	Sedum
Sollya heterophylla	Bluebell creeper
Tagetes erecti	Aztec marigold
Thalictrum polycarpum	Meadow-rue
Thymus vulgaris cvs.	Common thyme
Trichostema lanatum	Woolly blue-curls
Verbena cvs.	Verbena
Zantedeschia aethiopica	Calla-lilly
Zauschneria californica	California-fuchsia

111

We are indebted to Shirley A. Kerins, ASLA, horticultural consultant to Huntington Botanical Gardens, Pasadena and Curator of the Herb Garden, for this selection of plants.

gardens, gravel beds, containers, baskets or as color amid gray or green foliage shrubs. A to G, 5 to 9

Sedum *(Sedum* spp.) (See page 115.)

Spider-flower *(Cleome hasslerana)* is an annual or shrublike plant with pink or white flower clusters that grow up to 6 feet high. It is a good plant to use as a background against walls or fences. A to G, 5 to 9

GRASSES AND GROUND COVERS FOR EASY-CARE SURFACES

We have already discussed the high-water needs of conventional lawns and the advisability of reducing the lawn to a strip or smaller focal area or of replacing it with ground cover plants or hardscapes. Nevertheless, that is not always practical or desirable. Perhaps a lawn is something you just do not want to give up. Even though popular lawn grasses, such as Kentucky bluegrass, bent grass, ryegrass, and fescue, need more water than any other type of garden plant, drought-tolerant grasses, which require less water, could be used.

Drought-tolerant turf grasses will lie dormant in the winter and will turn brown; if this brown appearance does not appeal to you, you can buy a grass dye that will make the grass look green. In more mild areas, you also can seed a lawn in the fall for a winter lawn with a cool season annual grass, which requires much less water. When summer returns, the grass will die, but a fallow or dead grass still will keep down dust and prevent erosion. Drought-tolerant turf grasses include:

Bermuda grass *(Cynodon dactylon)* B G, 8 to 10; centipede grass *(Eremochloa ophiuroides)* B C F G, 8 to 10; St. Augustine grass *(Stenotaphrum secundatum)* B F G, 8 to 10; zoysia grass *(Zoysia* spp.) A B D E F G, 6 to 10; buffalo grass *(Buchloe dactyloides)* B C D F, 3 to 8; blue grama *(Boutelona gracilis)* B C D E, 3 to 8; smooth brome *(Bromus inermus)* A C D E, 3 to 8; and tall fescue *(Festuca arundinacea).* A C D E, 4 to 8

112

Drought-tolerant ornamental grasses and ground cover plants, which are described below, have some advantages over turf grasses. They have lower water demands, prevent erosion, reduce weeds by denying them light, cool the entire garden, and lessen the evaporation of water from the soil. They also give texture, form, and color to the landscape. With ornamental grasses, however, you usually need to have larger garden spaces because some species can become quite tall and wide spreading.

ORNAMENTAL GRASSES:

Big bluestem *(Andropogon gerardii)* is a hardy perennial grass and grows to 7 feet high. It is drought resistant and grows well in warmer climates. C D E F G, 3 to 9 Little bluestem *(A. scoparius)* only grows to 3 feet high, but is a good plant in large garden beds. A to G, 3 to 8

Blue fescue *(Festuca ovina* var. *glauca)* is a perennial grass and grows to 12 inches high with taller plumes. It is quite hardy and has silvery blue evergreen foliage. It is a good grass to use as edging in a mixed border. A B C D E G, 3 to 8

Eulalia grass *(Miscanthus sinensis)* is a slow growing (4 to 10 feet high) perennial grass and grows well in good garden soil and full sun. It is an excellent ornamental and is the best choice for northern regions. It has several cultivars with various color combinations: zebra grass ('Zebrinus'), maiden grass ('Gracillimus'), and striped eulalia ('Variegatus'). A C D E G, 3 to 8

Fountain grass *(Pennisetum setaceum)* is a tender perennial grass that grows in dense clumps to 4 feet high. It is very attractive with copper, pink, or purplish, fuzzy flower spikes and grows in any soil, but should be protected in the winter in northern climates. Plant as a focal point amid low shrubs or in gravel beds. A B F G, 6 to 10

Giant reed *(Arundo donax)* is the tallest of the perennial ornamental grasses, growing to 8 to 20 feet high. It has bright green leaves and reddish plumes, which turn silvery gray late in the season. It is hardy, but needs protection in colder climates. Use as a single focus plant in a large bed or as background. A B F G, 5 to 10

Pampas grass *(Cortaderia selloana)* is a perennial ornamental grass and grows to 20 feet high with towering white- or pink-flowered plumes. It is a very hardy plant in warm climates only and is often used as a windbreak in desert areas. B F G, 8 to 10

113

Plume grass *(Erianthus ravennae)* is a perennial ornamental grass or an annual in the North. It resembles pampas grass, but is less showy and only grows to 5 to 12 feet high. It is hardier than pampas grass and can be used in a perennial flower bed or shrub border. A B E F G, 5 to 10

GROUND COVERS:

Baby-sun-rose *(Aptenia cordifolia)* is a shrubby perennial succulent with trailing stems and fleshy leaves. It is for warmer climates only. It has red-purple blooms and trails nicely down walls, rock gardens, and hanging pots. B G, 10

Bearberry *(Arctostaphlos uva-ursi)* is an evergreen ground cover with leatherlike leaves, small rosy flowers, and brownish red berries. It can be grown in many types of soil and is very drought tolerant. It is an excellent ground cover for northern regions and can be successfully used in seaside areas. A C D E, 2 to 5

Coprosma *(Coprosma x kirkii)* makes a dense, hardy ground cover in dry soils. It is a tender evergreen shrub that grows to 18 inches high with yellow-green leaves and stems that lie flat. It is very drought tolerant and only can be successfully grown in hot dry climates. B F G, 8 to 10

Cotoneaster *(Cotoneaster microphyllus)* is a dwarf evergreen shrub that spreads about 6 feet wide and 2 feet high with small, dark green leaves. It is an excellent weed killer. Use on banks or to give a contoured look. A to G, 6 to 9

Coyote brush *(Baccharis pilularis)* is a California native evergreen shrub and is very dependable as a ground cover in desert areas. It makes a bright green wave or billowlike mat that spreads to over 6 feet wide and 8 to 24 inches high. B F G, 6 to 9

Evening-primrose *(Oenothera spp.)* are annuals, biennials and perennials that are good, showy ground covers for dry slopes. They have beautiful, rose pink to bright yellow flowers and grow to 1 to 3 feet high. A to G, 4 to 10 Mexican evening-primrose *(O. berlandieri)* is very hardy. B F G, 6 to 10

Gazania *(Gazania spp.)* are low growing annuals or perennials. Principal species include *G. ringens* (clumping type) and *G. uniflora* (trailing type); both species have single- or multicolored, attractive flowers. A B F G, 7 to 10

Horseshoe-vetch *(Hippocrepis comosa)* is a perennial ground cover that takes light foot traffic. It forms a 3-inch-high mat with golden yellow leaves. It is a good lawn substitute and can be mowed. A to G, 5 to 10

Juniper *(Juniperus* spp.*)* are evergreen shrubs for any garden situation. For ground cover ask for *J. prostrata* A to G, 3 to 8; *J. procumbens* A to G, 4 to 10; or *J. communis depressa* cvs. 'plumosa'. A to G, 4 to 9 *J. horizontalis* cvs. 'wiltonii' only grows to 4 inches high. A to G, 3 to 8

Lippia *(Phyla nodiflora* var. *rosea)* (sometimes still called *Lippia repens)* is a perennial that forms a flat, sturdy mat that tolerates foot traffic. Its multitude of small flowers attracts bees, so mow the flowers if you want to walk barefoot. It is a very good plant for desert areas, but lies dormant in the winter. A B F G, 9 to 10

Santolina *(Santolina* spp.*)* are evergreen subshrubs that grow to 2 feet high. Use for banks, ground covers, very low hedges, or borders. They grow in any soil, but may die to ground level in cold areas, returning in the spring. B F G, 7 to 10

Sedum *(Sedum* spp.*)* are low perennial succulents or subshrubs. They are among the hardiest of succulents with more than two dozen species that survive in many hardiness zones — at least twelve of these species can be used as ground covers, such as *S. x rubrotinctum.* They are good plants around swimming pools, but will not survive any foot traffic. A to G, 4 to 10

Snow-in-summer *(Cerastium tomentosum)* is a perennial that grows well in mild or cold climates and spreads dense mats of silvery gray leaves with masses of snow white flowers. It grows to 6 to 8 inches and is a good ground cover for banks or level ground. It also makes a great cascading plant for large containers, tops of walls, or as a fill-in between other plants. A to G, 2 to 9

Verbena *(Verbena* spp.*)* are perennials in warm climates and annuals in colder climates and thrive only in direct sun and heat. They are very drought resistant and when planted as annuals, bloom in four months from seed. *V. rigida* is a fast growing ground cover with dark green leaves and lilac to purple flowers. It grows to 10 to 20 inches high. A to G, 5 to 9

115

Low Water-Use Plant Selection

VINES FOR DRAMATIC BEAUTY

Ornamental vines happen to be among the most decorative and functional of plant forms. With good control, they can be used beneficially in the water-conserving landscape. Since vines not only climb walls, fences, and trellises, but also will spread across the ground, they also can serve as excellent ground covers. There are many species of vines, both native and imported, that have adapted to almost any climatic zone. The following is a selection of the most drought-resistant species that are suitable for the xeriscape garden.

Blood-trumpet *(Distictis buccinatoria)* is one of several evergreen *Distictis* vines with 4-inch-long, red flowers with yellow throats (formerly named *Bignonia*). B F G, 10 There are also trumpet vine species that are suitable for cold winter climates: crossvine *(Bignonia capreolata)* and trumpet vine *(Campsis radicans)*, which is native to the eastern United States. A to G, 6 to 9

Bougainvillea *(Bougainvillea* spp.*)* are some of the most beautiful and colorful of the tropical evergreen vines, but are not vines for cold winter climates. They will survive limited frost damage if grown against a warm wall. If not trained and pruned to a wall or terrace, they will spread out as a ground cover or form into a loose, sprawling shrub. B F G, 10

Cape-honeysuckle *(Tecomaria capensis)* is an evergreen vine from South Africa that thrives in sun and heat. It cannot be grown in cold winter climates. It has very fine, dark green-textured foliage with brilliant orange and red tubular blossoms. It also can be used as a ground cover for banks or steep slopes. B F G, 9 to 10

Cat's-claw *(Macfadyena unguis-cati)* is a partly deciduous vine that loses its leaves in cold winters. It is a very high, fast climber that grows to 25 to 40 feet with yellow trumpet flowers. B F G, 9 to 10

Cup-of-gold *(Solandra guttata)* is an evergreen vine that resists fog, salt spray, and wind. It is a very fast grower with broad, glossy leaves and golden yellow flowers with purple spots. It has sprawling growth to 40 feet. If you live along the Pacific Coast, this evergreen vine is for you. B G, 10

Euonymus *(Euonymus fortunei)* (See page 102.)

Grape ivy *(Cissus trifoliata)* is a low climbing deciduous vine that is related to Virginia creeper and is easy to grow in almost any soil. It is very woodsy looking with luscious, green leaves and is drought resistant. B G, 10

Grapevine *(Vitis spp.)* are deciduous vines for ornamental, fruit, wine, or shade purposes with species that will grow in almost any climate. The European vines *(Vitis vinifera)* are generally more drought tolerant. Grapevines make an excellent arbor or shade over a walkway, deck, or terrace; they even look good when they are dormant because of their thick, twining, gnarled branches. A to G, 5 to 10

Potato vine *(Solanum jasminoides)* is an evergreen or deciduous vine, depending on winter temperature. It has clusters of long blooming, white flowers and is a very fast growing vine. B F G, 9 to 10

Virgin's-bower *(Clematis ligustifolia)* is a small-flowered woody vine that grows to 20 feet high. Its flowers are very aromatic with beautiful plumed seed heads. A to G, 3 to 9

Wisteria *(Wisteria spp.)* are woody deciduous vines that are very long-lived and will grow to tremendous size if allowed. They are very beautiful with purple/blue/violet flowers that do, however, take a few years to bloom. Japanese wisteria *(W. floribunda)* has varieties with flowers in shades of pink, white, blue, purple, and lavender. They can be trained along a fence or arbor and can reach 100 feet or more. B F G, 5 to 10

VEGETABLES FOR HEALTHY EATING

Vegetables usually require plenty of water to grow, but there is no need to forsake their wonderful taste just to save water. If you install drip irrigation (see Chapter Six), you can reduce the amount of water that normally is applied to a vegetable garden by hose, sprinkler, or flood irrigation by as much as 70 percent. Because drip irrigation gets the water to the root zone, you will have less problems with weeds and will have an increase in productivity over conventional watering methods. Nevertheless, an alternative to the drip system for vegetables is soaker tubing or drip tape. Drip tape is a flattened tube that is laid along the rows of vegetables and trickles water into the soil. With either system,

117

water your vegetables preferably in early morning or late afternoon when evaporation will be minimal.

There are some low-water-use vegetables, but not many: cylindra beets, tepary beans, Desert King watermelons, Hopi orange lima beans, Swiss chard, and Hopi blue corn. The most water-loving vegetables are ordinary lettuce, carrots, melons, spinach, and standard yellow corn. Among less water-loving vegetables are green peppers, purple cauliflower, cabbage, broccoli, eggplant, tomatoes, squash, beets, and herbs, such as sage, rosemary, and thyme.

It may require a little searching, but try to buy traditional or "heirloom" seeds. Hybrid seeds, which are usually the only kind that you can buy in most nurseries, require more water and are genetically weaker than traditional nonhybrid vegetables. Hybrid vegetables are bred for fast growth in a short space of time. Traditional or heirloom seeds provide maximum nutritional benefits, have stronger genetic lines, give long-term yields, and most are naturally drought resistant.

Mulching also will reduce water needs considerably for vegetables. You will have to experiment for yourself, but by using a good moisture-retaining mulch around vegetables, you can cut back watering to once every two days. (See Chapter Five for appropriate mulches.)

Make a slight depression in the mulch mound that surrounds your vegetables to retain water.

Water-Conserving Gardens and Landscapes

PLANT SELECTION GUIDE

Common Name *Genus*	Recommended Species	Regions	Hardiness Zones
Trees or shrubs (see pages 94–101)			
Acacia *Acacia*	*A. longifolia* *A. armata*	B F G B F G	9–10 9–10
Australian-pine *Casuarina*	*C. cunninghamiana*	B F G	10
Australian-willow *Geijera*	*G. parviflora*	B F G	9–10
Bottletree *Brachychiton*	*B. populneus*	B	9–10
California Black Walnut *Juglans*	*J. hindsii*	A B	8–10
California Buckeye *Aesculus*	*A. californica*	A B	8–10
Carob *Ceratonia*	*C. siliqua*	B	10
Cedar *Cedrus*	*C. deodara*	A–G	6–9
Chinaberry *Melia*	*M. azedarach*	B F	9–10
Cypress *Cupressus*	*C. forbesii* *C. glabra* *C. macrocarpa* *C. sempervirens*	B G A B G B G A B G	9–10 8–10 8–10 8–10
Elm *Ulmus*	*U. pumila*	A–F	4–9

Low-Water-Use Plant Selection

Eucalyptus				
Eucalyptus	*E. preissiana*	B F G	9–10	
	E. caesia	B F G	9–10	
	E. macrocarpa	B F G	9–10	
	E. citriodora	B F G	9–10	
Fig				
Ficus		B F G	10	
Floss-silk tree				
Chorisia	*C. speciosa*	B G	9–10	
Golden raintree				
Koelreuteria	*K. paniculata*	A B F G	5–9	
Grevillea				
Grevillea		B G	10	
Hackberry				
Celtis	*C. occidentalis*	A–G	4–9	
Ironwood				
Lyonothamnus	*L. floribundus asplenifolius*	B G	10	
Jacaranda				
Jacaranda	*J. mimosifolia*	B F G	10	
Jerusalem thorn				
Parkinsonia	*P. aculeata*	B F G	9–10	
Jujube				
Ziziphus	*Z. jujuba*	B	10	
Kentucky coffee tree				
Gymnocladus	*G. dioica*	A B E G	5–9	
Linden				
Tilia	*T. tomentosa*	A–C E–G	5–9	
Locust				
Robinia	*R. x ambigua*	A–G	4–9	
	R. neomexicana	A-G	4-9	

120

Water-Conserving Gardens and Landscapes

Loquat			
Eriobotrya	*E. japonica*	A B F G	8–10
Mexican blue palm			
Brahea	*B. armata*	B F G	9–10
Oak			
Quercus		A B D–G	4–9
Olive			
Olea	*O. europaea*	B F G	8–10
Osage-orange			
Maclura	*M. pomifera*	A B D–G	5–9
Palm			
Chamaerops		B F G	9–10
Phoenix		B F G	9–10
Washingtonia		B F G	10
Palo verde			
Cercidium	*C. floridum*	B	9–10
Pepper tree			
Schinus	*S. molle*	B F G	9–10
	S. terebinthifolius	B F G	9–10
Pine			
Pinus	*P. pinea*	B F G	8–10
	P. thunbergiana	A–G	5–9
	P. ponderosa	A B C	5–9
Pistache			
Pistacia	*P. vera*	B F G	9–10
	P. chinenis	B F G	9–10
Redbud			
Cercis	*C. occidentalis*	A B E–G	7–9
Silk tree			
Albizia	*A. julibrissin*	B F G	5–10
Sumac			
Rhus	*R. lancea*	B F G	8–10

121

Low-Water-Use Plant Selection

Tamarisk *Tamarix*	*T. aphylla*	B F G	9–10
Tristania *Tristania*		B F G	9–10
Umbrella tree *Melia*	*M. azedarach*	A B F G	9–10

Shrubs (see pages 101–107)

Apache-plume *Fallugia*	*F. paradoxa*	B F	6–9
Artemisia *Artemisia*	*A. tridentata* *A. filifolia* *A. cana*	A B C F B C D F A B C	4–10 5–10 4–10
Bottlebrush *Callistemon*	*C. citrinus*	B F G	9–10
California holly grape *Mahonia*	*M. pinnata*	A B F G	7–10
Cape plumbago *Plumago*	*P. auriculata*	B F G	9–10
Cotoneaster *Cotoneaster*		A–G	5–9
Coyote brush *Baccharis*	*B. pilularis*	B F G	6–9
Crape-myrtle *Lagerstroemia*	*L. indica*	B F G	7–10
Elaeagnus *Elaeagnus*	*E. commutata*	A–G	3–9
Euonymus *Euonymus*		A–G	4–9

122

Water-Conserving Gardens and Landscapes

Flannelbush *Fremontodendron*	*F. californicum*	B C F	9–10
Germander *Teucrium*		A B E–G	7–10
Grevillea *Grevillea*	*G. thelamanniana*	B F G	10
Hopbush *Dodonaea*	*D. cuneata*	B F G	8–10
Juniper *Juniperus*		A–G	3–10
Lavender *Lavandula*		A B E–G	7–9
Leadplant *Amorpha*	*A. canescens*	A B D–G	3–7
Manzanita *Arctostaphylos*		A B	7–10
Mountain-mahogany *Cercocarpus*	*C. montanus*	A–C F	4–9
Mesquite *Prosopis*	*P. glandulosa torreyana*	B C F	5–9
Myrtle *Myrtus*		B F G	8–10
Nanking cherry *Prunus*	*P. tomentosa* *P. besseyi*	A–G A–G	3–9 3–9
Oleander *Nerium*	*N. oleander*	B F G	9–10
Photinia *Photinia*	*P. serrulata*	B F G	7–10

Low-Water-Use Plant Selection

Piñon pine *Pinus*	*P. edulis*	A–D F	4–9
Poinciana *Caesalpinia*	*C. gilliesii*	B G	10
Pomegranate *Punica*	*P. granatum*	B G	9–10
Rockrose *Cistus*		A B F G	7–10
Rose *Rosa*	*R. rugosa*	A–G	2–9
	R. foetida	A–G	2–9
	R. rubrifolia	A–G	2–9
	R. woodsii	A–G	2–9
Rosemary *Rosmarinus*	*R. officinalis*	A–G	7–10
Sage *Salvia*	*S. leucantha*	B F G	9–10
	S. greggi	B F G	9–10
Saltbush *Atriplex*	*A. canescens*	A–D F	4–10
	A. lentiformus	A–D F	4–10
Silk-tassel bush *Garrya*	*G. fremontii*	A B F G	8–10
Xylosma *Xylosma*	*X. congestum*	A B F G	8–10
Yucca *Yucca*	*Y. aloifolia*	B C F	6–9
	Y. baccata	B C F	5–9
	Y. glauca	C D F	4–9
	Y. elata	B C F	6–10
	Y. whipplei	B	9–10

Water-Conserving Gardens and Landscapes

Perennials and annuals (see pages 107–112)

Agave *Agave*		B F G	7–10
Aloe *Aloe*	*A. arborescens*	A G	10
Anacyclus *Anacyclus*	*A. depressus*	A B C F	6– 9
Belladonna *Amaryllis*		A B F G	5–10
Blue-eyed-grass *Sisyrinchium*	*S. bellum*	B G	9–10
Buckwheat *Eriogonum*		A–D F G	4–10
Capeweed *Arctotheca*	*A. calendula*	A B F G	8
Coreopsis *Coreopsis*	*C. lanceolata* *C. tinctoria*	A–G A–G	5–9 5–9
Cosmos *Cosmos*		A–G	5–9
Dudleya *Dudleya*		B G	10
Echeveria *Echeveria*		B G	10
Euryops *Euryops*		B G	9–10
Evening-primrose *Oenothera*		A–G	4–10

125

Flax			
Linum	L. perenne	A–G	4–10
	L. lewisii	A–G	4–10
Gaillardia			
Gaillardia	G. pulchella	A–G	4–9
	G. aristata	A–G	4–9
Gay-feather			
Liatris		D E F G	4–9
Horehound			
Marrubium	M. vulgare	A–G	4–9
Indigo			
Baptisia	B. australis	E G	5–9
Iceplant			
Mesembryanthemum		B G	9–10
Iris			
Iris		A–G	2–9
Jerusalem-sage			
Phlomis	P. fructicosa	B F G	7
Lion's-ear			
Leonotis	L. leonuris	B G	10
Matilija poppy			
Romneya	R. coulteri	A B	9–10
Mexican-sunflower			
Tithonia	T. rotundifolia	A–G	5–9
New-Zealand-flax			
Phormium	P. tenax	B F G	9–10
Puya			
Puya	P. berteroniana	B G	9–10
Red valerian			
Centranthus	C. ruber	A–G	5–9

Water-Conserving Gardens and Landscapes

Rose-moss
Portulaca   *P. grandiflora*   A–G   5–9

Sedum
Sedum   A–G   4–10

Spider-flower
Cleome   *C. hasslerana*   A–G   5–9

Turf grasses (see page 112)

Bermuda grass
Cynodon   *C. dactylon*   B G   8–10

Blue grama
Boutelona   *B. gracilis*   B C D E   3–8

Buffalo grass
Buchloe   *B. dactyloides*   B C D F   3–8

Centipede grass
Eremochloa   *E. ophiuroides*   B C F G   8–10

Smooth brome
Bromus   *B. inermus*   A C D E   3–8

St. Augustine grass
Stenotaphrum   *S. secundatum*   B F G   8–10

Tall fescue
Festuca   *F. arundinacea*   A C D E   4–8

Zoysia grass
Zoysia   A B D–G   6–10

Ornamental grasses (see pages 113–114)

Bluestem
Andropogon   *A. gerardii*   C–G   3–9
                     A. scoparius   A–G   3–8

Blue fescue
Festuca   *F. ovina* var. *glauca* A–E G   3–8

Low-Water-Use Plant Selection

Eulalia grass Miscanthus	M. sinensis	A C–E G	3–8
Fountain grass Pennisetum	P. setaceum	A B F G	6–10
Giant reed Arundo	A. donax	A B F G	5–10
Pampas grass Cortaderia	C. selloana	B F G	8–10
Plume grass Erianthus	E. ravennae	A B E–G	5–10

Ground covers (see pages 114–115)

Baby-sun-rose Aptenia	A. cordifolia	B G	10
Bearberry Arctostaphlos	A. uva-ursi	A C D E	2–5
Coprosma Coprosma	C. x kirkii	B F G	8–10
Cotoneaster Cotoneaster	C. microphyllus	A–G	6–9
Coyote brush Baccharis	B. pilularis	B F G	6–9
Evening-primrose Oenothera	O. berlandieri	B F G	6–10
Gazania Gazania	G. ringens	A B F G	7–10
	G. uniflora	A B F G	7–10
Horseshoe-vetch Hippocrepis	H. comosa	A–G	5–10

Juniper			
Juniperus	*J. prostrata*	A–G	3–8
	J. procumbens	A–G	4–10
	J. communis depressa		
	cvs. 'plumosa'	A–G	3–9
	J. horizontalis cvs.	A–G	3–8
	'wiltonii'		
Lippia			
Phyla	*P. nodiflora* var.		
	rosea	A B F G	9–10
Santolina		B F G	7–10
Sedum			
Sedum	*S.* x *rubrotinctum*	B F G	9–10
Snow in-summer			
Cerastium	*C. tomentosum*	A–G	2–9
Verbena			
Verbena	*V. rigida*	A–G	5–9

Vines (see pages 116–117)

Blood-trumpet			
Distictis	*D. buccinatoria*	B F G	10
Bougainvillea			
Bougainvillea		B F G	10
Cape-honeysuckle			
Tecomaria	*T. capensis*	B F G	9–10
Cat's-claw			
Macfadyena	*M. unguis-cati*	B F G	9–10
Crossvine			
Bignonia	*B. capreolata*	A–G	6–9
Cup-of-gold			
Solandra	*S. guttata*	B G	10

129

Low-Water-Use Plant Selection

Euonymus *Euonymus*	*E. fortunei*	A–G	4–9
Grape ivy *Cissus*	*C. trifoliata*	B G	10
Grapevine *Vitis*	*V. vinifera*	A–G	5–10
Potato vine *Solanum*	*S. jasminoides*	B F G	9–10
Trumpet vine *Campsis*	*C. radicans*	A–G	6–9
Virgin's-bower *Clematis*	*C. ligustifolia*	A–G	3–9
Wisteria *Wisteria*	*W. floribunda*	B F G	5–10

The region and hardiness designations are general guidelines. Consult your local nursery owner for detailed information on selected plants.

Water-Conserving Gardens and Landscapes

CHAPTER EIGHT

TENDING THE XERISCAPE GARDEN

PLANTING ALTERNATIVES • INSECT & DISEASE CONTROL • WEED PREVENTION

The basics of xeriscape landscaping are good design, thorough soil preparation, low-water-use plants, zoning plants by water requirements, an efficient irrigation system, mulching of plants and shrubs, and timely maintenance.

Of course you could do what my friend did. He simply paved over the entire area that surrounded his house with flagstones, brick, and wooden decks. For greenery and color, he used large containers and strategically placed pots that included large cast concrete containers to hold trees. He certainly has a low-water-use garden. But some people want landscaping that is a little more integrated with plants, shrubs, or trees.

The surprising thing about water-conserving landscaping, though, is that you can use a great deal of hardscape (brick or gravel pathways, patios, and wooden decks) and still achieve the effect of a lush, natural looking landscape.

PLANTING ALTERNATIVES

Raised beds. For those with poor soil or a flat, uninteresting garden area, building raised beds is a practical and aesthetically pleasing solution. These raised beds can be of different heights to add contour to a flat area or to create small minigardens or miniature canyons. They can be built from a variety of materials, such as old bricks, concrete blocks, or old railroad ties. Raised beds, boxes, and containers bring order to a garden. Plants are also easier to tend and can be more productive than their ground-dwelling counterparts.

A very cost-effective and environmentally-smart way to use raised beds is to build them with walls of recycled concrete. The rough, irregular surface of the recycled concrete works very well in a garden setting.

Wooden raised bed containers are also excellent for growing intensive crops of vegetables and flowers. They can be used on steep slopes to create a terrace effect when set back into the slope; this placement eliminates the problem of water and soil runoff. Another advantage is the pH level of the soil easily can be controlled to suit the plants.

These wooden containers can be almost any size, but they are unwieldy if they are larger than about 4 feet wide by 6 or 8 feet long; that is large enough to grow vegetables for a family or a fine display of annuals. Construct the container with a depth of 12 to 14 inches, which will be deep enough even for root vegetables. Nail 1-inch chicken wire over the bottom to keep out moles and rodents. Cedar, cypress, or redwood planks that are reinforced at the corners and fastened with galvanized nails or screws will last for years. These containers also can be turned into cold frames by covering them with large pieces of plastic or glass.

Containers. Decks, patios, and paving (stone or aggregates) in the xeriscape garden make ideal staging areas for tubs, pots, and other containers. Container gardening is an obvious way to save water since little or no water is lost to the surrounding soil. With drip irrigation, the chore of watering each pot is eliminated (see Chapter Six).

The biggest problem with containers is the accumulation of salts. When these salts become obvious as a white, chalkish deposit on the bottom and sides of the container, it is time to leach either by repeated watering or by plunging smaller pots into water, preferably rainwater or water that has been filtered.

To avoid having to water daily, make sure the pots are big enough to provide plenty of soil around the root ball. A plant can grow about three times as high as its container and up to twice the width before it needs repotting. When the plant outgrows the pot, all the soil is taken up by the root system, and there is no room for moisture to accumulate. Overgrown plants dry out very quickly after watering. In very hot climates, reduce moisture loss by placing a smaller pot inside a larger pot and fill the gap between them with sand.

Ask your local nursery owner about suitable plants for tubs and containers. Dwarf citrus varieties do very well in containers, and evergreens grow better in containers than deciduous trees because of their more compact root systems.

New-Zealand-flax *(Phormium tenax)* does well in containers and its long, sword shaped leaves grow tall and make a very full display. Woody perennials, such as English lavender *(Lavandula augustifolia)*, do well in containers as do dwarf bamboo *(Arundinaria pumila)* and most bulbs and annuals (see pages 107 to 112). Most herbs, heliotrope *(Heliotropium* spp.*)*, bromelia *(Bromelia* spp.*)*, bouvardia *(Bouvardia* spp.*)*, and aspidistra *(Aspidistra* spp.*)* fare well in containers.

You will have to adjust your drip irrigation system to different container sizes by adding or removing emitters (see Chapter Six). If you do not use a drip irrigation system, remember to leave at least 3 inches of space between the soil and the pot rim for watering by hand.

Danger Signals from Container Plants

Because of the limited amount of soil in a container, you must watch out for signs of salt buildup, which can injure or kill the plant. Salts, such as alkali, are present in water and gradually build up in the soil.

By the time there is a white, chalky deposit on the rim or bottom of the container, and leaf edges start to turn brown, salt buildup has already begun to damage the plant. To leach out the alkali and other salts, take the container outside or place it in a sink. Water the plant thoroughly until water runs from the drainage holes. Repeat this watering at least four times. Replace the nutrients that have been washed away with the salts with your favorite container plant fertilizer. Mix the fertilizer with water at half the recommended strength if the plant previously was grown in the garden.

INSECT & DISEASE CONTROL

If you have not already switched from chemical to biological control methods against insects in your garden, I strongly suggest that you do switch when you install water-conserving landscaping. The hazards of chemical pesticides have been known since 1962 when Rachel Carson blew the whistle on DDT and other pesticides in her book *Silent Spring,* which launched the environmental movement.

Contamination of water supplies that was caused by pesticide residues is common throughout the nation, but especially in states with large farming and agricultural areas. Pesticides are not effective against many insects because the insects have become immune to them. The biggest drawback to pesticides is that they also kill all the beneficial insects that normally keep the damaging insects under control. With fewer predators around, there is a resurgence of the pests that you were trying to kill, often in overwhelming numbers.

Available today are numerous biological pest controls and non-toxic methods of handling many garden pests. Water that is sprayed with force directly at the infestation can wash away some insects. A soap spray also is often very effective against aphids and other pests (see below). The best controls, though, are biological — ladybugs, praying mantises, parasitic wasps, spiders, and common black ground beetles. One ladybug, for instance, will eat about 5,000 aphids over its lifespan.

Soap sprays

Soap sprays are safe preparations and are very effective against a variety of soft-bodied insects. Aphids, mealybugs, spider mites, spittlebugs, stinkbugs, crickets, and grasshoppers can all be washed away by a soap spray. Mix 3 tablespoons of mild soap, such as Fels Naptha, Ivory Snow (the powdered soap), or Safer's Insecticidal Soap to 1 gallon of water. (Do not use any type of laundry detergent.) Apply the spray to the foliage with a hand sprayer. To kill the insects requires a direct hit, so spraying must be repeated often. Note: Stronger concentrations of soap are no more effective at killing insects, but can cause *significant* plant damage.

Trichogramma is a parasitic wasp that destroys the eggs of cabbageworms, cabbage loopers, geranium budworms, and corn earworms. Cryptolaemus beetles prey on mealybugs. Aphytis wasps are parasitic on scale insects. Tiny encarsia wasps prey on whiteflies.

Lacewings and lacewing larvae dine happily on aphids, mites, mealybugs, cabbageworms, cabbage loopers, corn earworms, and geranium budworms. Persimilis is a nonsucking, harmless mite that eats pest mites. Ask your local nursery or garden supply store for names of biological control companies in your area, or see the Source List on pages 149 to 150.

A combination of biological insect controls and the use of insect-repelling plants (parsley and garlic, for instance, discourage aphids) is known as the bio-control method and is fully covered in books, such as *The Bug Book: Harmless Insect Controls* by John and Helen Philbrick (Garden Way Publishing, 1974), *Down-to-Earth Gardening Know-How for the '90s* by Dick Raymond (Storey Publishing, 1991), and *Bugs, Slugs & Other Thugs: Controlling Garden Pests Organically* by Rhonda Massingham Hart (Storey Publishing, 1991).

Remember that every bug is not dedicated to destroying your garden. Many are very beneficial. Without them, pollination could not occur. There is a natural, close relationship (symbiotic) between plants, insects, and insect predators, including frogs, toads, lizards, and birds. In a well-balanced and well-maintained garden, a natural control process is at work. Only when that balance is upset, as when beneficial insects are destroyed by chemical sprays or when birds, lizards, and other predators are discouraged, do you then have uncontrollable population explosions of harmful insects.

In the xeriscape garden, many of the plants are naturally resistant to disease and insect damage, especially those from our native wild plant stock. Plants in good condition that receive adequate moisture have built-in defense mechanisms. It is when a plant has been damaged by under- or overwatering, excessive fertilizer use, or otherwise abused that the door is open to destructive insects and disease.

Insects love overcrowded gardens with plenty of humid shade. Fortunately, the more open design of the low-water-use garden permits good air circulation and sunshine to discourage insect population explosions. Be sure to place your plants in their most suitable location. If you plant a shade lover in sunshine or vice versa, that plant will sicken and likely die; if not on its own, then helped along by insects or disease.

The secret of insect and disease control is timeliness. Most insect problems can be handled in the early stages with little more than a

Tips for Battling Insects

The key to insect control is knowledge, not chemicals. Many insects are beneficial to the gardener not only by helping plants to propagate, but also by eating the few species that do eat and attack your plants. Remember, spraying kills the good guys and the bad guys.

Good guys include ladybugs, wasps, spiders, praying mantises, ground beetles, dragonflies, lightning bugs, and syrphid flies. Commercial suppliers of ladybugs and praying mantises can provide information on the proper number of these beneficial insects needed for your area (see Source List on pages 149 to 150).

1. If you see 1-inch-long, brown, sticky clumps on the twigs of trees or shrubs in the winter, do not remove them; they are the egg cases of the praying mantis and can contain up to 100 eggs in each case. When they are young, praying mantises will devour aphids, spider mites, and other pests before graduating to larger prey.

2. The tiny eggs of the lacewing stand up from leaves on delicate stalks, like miniature sprouts. Do not destroy these eggs because lacewings are voracious eaters of many pests, such as aphids, mealybugs, and leafhoppers.

3. Do not allow weed patches to build up at the edges of your garden; weed patches are often the source of insect infestations. Wrap sticky papers around the trunks of trees or shrubs if they are especially susceptible to insect attack.

4. Mothballs that are scattered around insect-prone plants emit sufficient odor to keep away many insects.

5. If you have fruit trees, pick up all fallen fruit promptly. Make a very efficient trap for fruit beetles by putting pieces of decaying fruit in a glass jar. Tie a piece of aluminum screening over the top and cut a 1/2-inch hole in the screening. Place the trap 1 or 2 yards from the fruit tree.

6. If snails are a problem, try the beer trap. Pour 1 or 2 ounces of beer in a small can. Place the can on the ground on its side. The snails appear to love beer and as many as 20 or 30 will enter the can and stay until you dispose of them in the garbage.

Water-Conserving Gardens and Landscapes

7. A roll of damp newspaper that is tied with string and laid on the ground is one of the best traps for earwigs and pill bugs. They crawl in the newspaper at dawn; you dispose of them in late morning.
8. Spraying plants occasionally with a strong jet of water will remove many pests.

vigorous spraying of water. Check plants regularly. If you have a compost pile, locate it as far away as possible from the garden. Many insects, such as earwigs and bacterial plant disease organisms, thrive on decaying organic material, so do not leave dead plants, weeds, or plant cuttings lying about the garden. If a plant looks sick, take a cutting of the plant to your local nursery or garden center, a neighborhood garden expert, or a county extension agent and ask their advice. (Wash off the cutting first and place it in a plastic bag.)

Sometimes a plant has been weakened and, consequently, is susceptible to insect infestations or blight. It would be wise to remove it from the garden before it can infect others. If it is an expensive plant or one that you really want to save, you might try transplanting it to another section of the garden. It could be that the soil conditions or lighting were not optimum for that plant. You also could experiment by placing a difficult plant in a container or box where you could adjust the soil conditions to its requirements and could experiment with varying locations of shade and light. This is especially useful if you are contemplating an entire bed of similar plants and want to be sure that they will thrive before investing in them.

A special note to desert gardeners: There is a soil fungus called Texas root rot that is frequently a serious problem for gardeners in Arizona, California, Nevada, New Mexico, and Texas. Texas root rot is the common name for *Phymotochrichum omnivorum*. It attacks and kills all woody plants that are not rot resistant. The fungus is also known as cotton root rot because it became widespread in cotton-farming land. Once it attacks a plant, death can be swift, or the plant can linger for several years as leaves and branches die.

137

Like most fungi, it is very hard to spot before serious damage has been done to the plant. Most experts say that this root rot spreads along the roots of plants by moving from one root system to another. Even when you know a tree has died from this fungus, it is still difficult to find the brownish ribbons of fungi on the plant; they look like flattened veins on the outside of the root.

Texas root rot thrives in warm, moist soil. It becomes particularly active after desert summer rains. In the garden, it seems to lie in wait until the plants are at their peak of stress from low humidity and hot temperatures. The symptoms of root rot are the sudden wilting of a branch or the whole tree and are not unlike those symptoms from overwatering or poor drainage. Various, pesky root borers, however, can also cause a whole tree or individual branches to wilt. Eliminate this possibility by cutting open pieces of a branch from the affected area and inspecting for root borers. You may find a borer still inside, but more likely you will find the channels that were cut through the twigs as the borers ate the nutrient-rich heart of the wood. Heat exhaustion, roots that are burned by fertilizer, or gophers that eat the roots will also cause the tree or parts of it to wilt.

With Texas root rot, though, often just one side of the tree wilts. Usually the leaves will wilt and turn brown, but will not fall from the tree as they normally do in the dormant season. The first thought of most gardeners is that the tree was not watered properly. Unfortunately if it is root rot, watering the tree makes things worse as the moisture encourages the fungi to grow.

For positive identification, it takes microscopic examination, which you can request from your local extension office. The extension agent will need a root sample about 1 foot long. Dig down and cut a length of any root that is about ¼ inch thick. Handle it carefully; do not wipe away the soil, or you could destroy the evidence. Wrap the root in damp newspapers and keep it moist; if it dries out, the fungi will fall away.

Once you know for sure that a plant has been attacked by Texas root rot, it is very difficult to save. The key to salvage is the knowledge that the fungi thrives in alkaline soil and dislikes acidic conditions. To be successful, though, any rescue attempt must be made as soon as the symptoms are suspected and confirmed. A few days delay can mean the difference between success and failure. You have to change the pH level of the soil where the roots lie and provide a rich dose of nutrients so that the plant can grow new and, hopefully, uninfected roots. Whenever a tree loses a good deal of its roots, you must compensate by severe trimming. Cut away all wilting branches since they will never recover. If you save the tree, the remaining branches will be sufficient for the tree to rebuild itself.

The next step is to change the pH level of the soil around the root zone from alkaline to acidic and to provide nutrients for the new root growth. Spread about 2 inches of good compost under the tree on all sides and extend it a little beyond the root line. Cow manure works well and has the advantage of being cheaper than a commercial compost from a nursery. On top of the spread manure, scatter ammonium sulphate, about 1 pound to every 10 square feet. (Do **not** substitute ammonium phosphate because it is not water soluble.) Follow the ammonium sulphate with soil sulphur, about 1 pound to every 10 square feet. Dig this mixture carefully into the soil to minimize damage to the tree roots. Do **not** make this mixture stronger. It is already a potent dose of strong chemicals since this is a last-ditch, throw-caution-to-the-winds kind of remedy.

The next step is to water the entire area thoroughly and deeply to take the nutrients down to the root zone. To do this quickly and thoroughly, build a small berm of soil around the tree to create a basin and either flood irrigate or set up a temporary sprinkler. You will need enough water to take the nutrients down at least 3 feet. About 10 days later, repeat the watering; then wait and hope that it worked.

While the manure provides nutrients for new root growth, the ammonium sulphate and soil sulphur create an acid reaction in the soil. Although one treatment of this acid-forming mixture appears to do the job for most plants, at least two authorities recommend such a treatment annually. This makes for good preventive medicine in a root rot area, but it is expensive and a lot of work.

If the tree dies despite your best efforts or nearby trees also become infected, you should not replant with anything but naturally rot-resistant species. Unfortunately there are not many choices. Equally unfortunate is some very favored trees are very susceptible, including stone fruit trees (peach, plum, almond, apricot), willows, elms, poplars, bottletree, cottonwoods, ginkgo, and drought-resistant species, such as fig and pepper trees. Shrubs that are equally susceptible include buddleias, cassias, castor bean, cotoneaster (silver-leaf), lilacs, photinia (Chinese), flowering quince, roses, silver-berry, and spirea.

Tree species that are immune to Texas root rot include most of the true bamboos, ornamental banana, and all species of palms. Immune shrubs are agaves, bird-of-paradise, draecena, pampas grass, giant reed, and yucca.

Resistant species of trees that can be planted in soil that has been treated as above or can be planted near known root rot locations include the following: aleppo pine, cedar elm, citrus (on sour orange rootstocks), Arizona, Italian, and Monterey eucalyptus, evergreen tamarisk, fruitless mulberry, mesquite, palo verde, American and Arizona sycamore, and native black walnut. Shrubs include cacti, crape-myrtle, Arizona elderberry, jasmine, juniper, oleander, pome-granate, pyrancantha, rosemary, Russian olive, and Siberian pea shrub.

You can obtain a complete guide to rot-resistant trees and shrubs from your area's extension service office. Your local nursery should also stock guides and should be able to lead you to resistant species.

No effective cure has been developed for Texas root rot infestation in the soil. It would take so many expensive and toxic chemicals to kill the fungus that the environment would be damaged severely. If your garden is infested, either learn to live with it by only planting immune or resistant species or use the solar soil sterilization method that is outlined in Chapter Four.

Gardeners in desert areas can take certain precautions to avoid accidentally bringing Texas root rot into their gardens:

- Do not accept free plant gifts without finding out where they have come from and why they are being given away.
- Do not gather leaf mold from beneath native mesquite trees for use in your compost. Mesquite trees often carry the disease, but like many carriers, they do not show any evidence of the disease themselves.
- Do not import topsoil from any area where cotton previously was grown.
- Do not buy container plants that originally were grown in local soil that could be infected; buy plants that were grown only in sterile mixtures.

Water-Conserving Gardens and Landscapes

WEED PREVENTION

What is a weed? Emerson said that a weed was a plant whose virtues have not yet been discovered. Or, as one of his contemporaries said, a weed is but a flower in disguise. That may be true, but weeds can make a mess of a garden. Because they have not been crossbred and refined, in most sunny gardens they are genetically hardier than most garden plants.

Weeds, like your favorite plants, also require light, air, water, and nutrients. Deny them those requirements, and the weeds will die. Mulches help by denying weeds the light that they need to grow. By using low-water-use drip irrigation, you also deny them the water that they need.

There are two techniques for preventing weed growth that work: 1. Smother them. 2. Cut off the tops of the weeds. To smother weeds, cut the weeds close to the ground, then lay down newspapers, cardboard, or black plastic and cover it with mulch or soil. The idea is to keep out both light and air. After several weeks, even the roots will be dead. This works for almost all weeds except certain parasitic vines that spread too widely to cover.

Where there are numerous outbreaks among established plants, smothering may not be practical. In this case, cut off the tops of the weeds close to the ground as the tops appear. If you continue cutting off the tops during the growing season, the roots will not be able to manufacture food without foliage, and they will die.

Nontoxic Weed Removal

Toxic weed killers contaminate the soil and underground water supplies as rains carry the chemicals down into the soil. You expose yourself and others to toxic fumes every time you use chemical herbicides. It is so much simpler to just pull up the weeds. The best time to remove weeds is after a rain or a watering when the soil is soft.

For difficult weeds between paving, patio stones, or brick, mix 1 cup of table salt in a $1/2$ gallon of hot water and pour enough of the salt solution in the cracks to reach the weed roots. Do **not** apply this elsewhere in the garden because the salts will build up and kill other plants.

141

Tending the Xeriscape Garden

Common weeds, such as lamb's-quarters, pigweed, purslane, and ragweed, are fairly easy to control through cultivation — pulling or digging them out of the soil. There are others, though, that can be extremely difficult to eradicate once they are established in the garden. Learn to recognize the real bad guys of the weed world — poison ivy, Canada thistle, Johnsongrass, quack grass, and bindweed. Johnsongrass and quack grass appear to grow as fast as you dig them out, and the only thing that seems to work, for a while, is smothering them (see page 141).

Weeding every ten days or two weeks should be sufficient to keep weeds under control unless there is a heavy rainfall. Check the garden one or two days after a heavy rain and remove any sprouting weeds. If you wait for one or two weeks, the job can become a major chore.

While it is true that weeds are simply plants that we do not wish to cultivate, the international traffic in plants has caused a serious problem for natural plant communities by introducing plants that are alien to the local ecosystem. The problem arises because once introduced, an alien plant frequently has no natural controls in its new environment. Plants in their home environment have usually been forced into narrowly defined ecological niches through a long evolutionary process that involves interaction with other plants, nutritional considerations, climate, and natural predators.

Alien plants that are introduced into a new environment are suddenly unburdened of these natural controls and spread wildly to the detriment of the local or native species. For instance, Japanese honeysuckle, kudzu vine, and Japanese knotweed are not a problem in their native lands. Since being introduced to North America, they have become common and pernicious perennial weeds, crowding out and strangling many native plants.

In China, the ailanthus is known as the tree-of-heaven because it grows where almost nothing else can grow and reaches a towering 75 feet at maturity, growing as much as 6 feet in a single season. It was imported to this country and put to very beneficial use in greening many cities across America. The problem is that ailanthus was allowed to spread into the country. Now it is a serious menace to valuable native tree species in New England, New York, Pennsylvania, and California where it has gone "wild," creating dense, junglelike thickets.

Water-Conserving Gardens and Landscapes

With the xeriscape garden concept, there is an opportunity to help correct this ecological imbalance by concentrating on the many drought-resistant native species of plants and trees, rather than bringing alien plants into one's backyard. This is not a plea for ecological isolationism, just a plea to use our native species whenever you can.

SOURCE LIST

NATIVE PLANT AND SEED SUPPLIERS

The following suppliers distribute by mail order or retail sales.
Write for catalogs or information.

The Theodore Payne Foundation
10459 Tuxford Street
Sun Valley, CA 91352

Blue Oak Nursery
2731 Mountain Oak Lane
Rescue, CA 95672

Wildflower Seed Company
Box 406
St. Helena, CA 94574

Bernardo Beach Native Plant Farm
Star Route 7, Box 145
Vequita, NM 87062

Dry Country Plants
3904 Highway 70 East
Las Cruces, NM 88001

New Mexico Cactus Research
Box 787, Dept 102
Belen, NM 87002
Cactus and succulents only

Plants of the Southwest
1812 Second Street
Santa Fe, NM 87501

Southwestern Native Seeds
Box 50503
Tucson, AZ 85703

Nichols Garden Nursery
1190 N. Pacific Highway
Albany, OR 97321

Territorial Seed Company
PO Box 27
80030 Territorial Road
Lorane, OR 97451
Vegetables for the Northwest

Gurney Seed & Nursery Co.
Dept. 98-4724 Page Street
Yankton, SD 57079

Inter-State Nurseries
Catalog Division
Louisiana, MO 63353

Stark Brothers Nurseries
Highway 54
Louisiana, MO 63353

Heritage Gardens
1 Meadow Ridge Road
Shenandoah, IA 51601

Earl May Seed & Nursery
208 N. Elm Street
Shenandoah, IA 51603

Kurt Bluemel Inc.
2740 Greene Lane
Baldwin, MD 21013
Ornamental grasses, bamboos

Comstock, Ferre & Co.
263 Main Street
PO Box 125
Wethersfield, CT 06109

Andre Viette Farm & Nursery
Route 1, Box 16
State Route 608
Fisherville, VA 22939

CANADIAN
McConnell Nurseries
Port Burwell, ON N0J 1T0
Canada

McFayden Seed Co.
30 Ninth Street, Box 1800
Brandon, MB R7A 6NA
Canada

W.H. Peron
515 Labelle Blvd.
Chomeday Laval, QC H7V 2T3
Canada

For information on other suppliers of native plants and seeds, write:
The Mailorder Association of Nurseries
Dept. SCI
8683 Doves Fly Way
Laurel, MD 20723
(301) 499-9143

PRODUCT SUPPLIER

Concrete Paver Systems, Inc.
8170 Beverly Blvd.
Los Angeles, CA 90048
213-658-8671

Planetary Solutions
P.O. Box 1049
Boulder, CO 80306-1049

INFORMATION ON XERISCAPING

National Xeriscape Council Inc.
PO Box 767936
Roswell, GA 30076-7936

PLANT SOCIETIES

The following organizations are special interest groups that focus on various aspects of cultivating native plants. Write for more information about native plants in your area.

Alabama Wildflower Society
Box 115
Northport, AL 35476

Arizona Native Plant Society
PO Box 41206 Sun Station
Tucson, AZ 85717

Colorado Native Plant Society
PO Box 200
Fort Collins, CO 80522

Connecticut Botanical Society
1 Livermore Trail
Killingworth, CT 06417

Florida Native Plant Society
1203 Orange Avenue
Winter Park, FL 32789

Georgia Botanical Society
1676 Andover Court
Doraville, GA 30360

Idaho Native Plant Society
Box 9451
Boise, ID 83706

Illinois Native Plant Society
Dept. of Botany
Southern Illinois University
Carbondale, IL 62901

Kansas Wildflower Society
Mulvane Art Center
Washburn University
17th & Jewell Street
Topeka, KS 66621

Louisiana Native Plant Society
PO Box 151
Saline, LA 71070

Minnesota Native Plant Society
202 N. Andrews Avenue
University of Minnesota
1445 Gortner Avenue
St. Paul, MN 55108

Mississippi Native Plant Society
202 N. Andrews Avenue
Cleveland, MS 38732

Missouri Native Plant Society
Box 6612
Jefferson City, MO 65102

Montana Native Plant Society
Biology Dept.
University of Montana
Missoula, MT 59812

New England Wildflower Society
Hemenway Road
Framingham, MA 01701

New Jersey Native Plant Society
Box 1295R
Morristown, NJ 07960

New York Torrey Botanical Club
New York Botanical Garden
Bronx, NY 10458

North Carolina Wildflower Preservation Society
UNC-CH Totten Center 457A
Chapel Hill, NC 27514

Ohio Native Plant Society
6 Louise Drive
Chagrin Falls, OH 44022

Native Plant Society of Oregon
Dept. of Biology
S. Oregon State College
Ashland, OR 97520

Pennsylvania Native Plant Society
1806 Commonwealth Building
316 4th Avenue
Pittsburgh, PA 15222

147

Philadelphia Botany Club
Academy of Natural Sciences
19th and Benjamin Franklin
Parkway
Philadelphia, PA 19103

Tennessee Native Plant Society
Dept. of Botany
University of Tennessee
Knoxville, TN 37916

Utah Native Plant Society
University of Utah
Building 436
Salt Lake City, UT 84112

Virginia Native Plant Society
PO Box 844 of Botany
Annandale, VA 22003

**Washington Native Plant
Society**
Department of Botany
University of Washington
Seattle, WA 98195

**West Virginia Native Plant
Society**
Brooks Hall
West Virginia University
Morgantown, WV 26506

Wyoming Native Plant Society
PO Box 1471
Cheyenne, WY 82003

LANDSCAPING INSTITUTES

*The following organizations
have specialized programs and/
or information resources relat-
ing to landscape design.*

**California State Polytechnic
University**
Institute for Environmental
Design
3801 West Temple Avenue
Pomona, CA 91768

Iowa State University
Design Research Institute
134 College of Design
Ames, IA 50011

**Landscape Architecture
Foundation**
1733 Connecticut Avenue NW
Washington, DC 20009

Louisiana State University
Information Systems Lab
Room 216, College of Design
Baton Rouge, LA 70803

University of Arizona
Arizona Agricultural Experi-
mental Station
Tucson, AZ 85717

**University of Guelph
Arboretum**
Guelph, ON N1G 2W1
Canada

148

University of Kentucky
Kentucky Agricultural
Experimental Station
Agricultural Sciences
Building North
Lexington, KY 40546

University of Michigan
Nichols Arboretum
Ann Arbor, MI 48109-1115

University of Pennsylvania
Morris Arboretum
9414 Meadowbrook Avenue
Philadelphia, PA 19118

Washington State University
College of Agriculture and Home
Economics Research Center
Pulman, WA 99164

BIOLOGICAL & ORGANIC GARDENING SUPPLIERS

Association of Applied Insect Ecologists
100 N. Winchester Blvd.
Suite 260
Santa Cruz, CA 95050
Beneficial insects

Bio-Control Company
PO Box 337
57A Zink Road
Berry Creek, CA 95916
Beneficial insects

Bio-Resources
PO Box 902
1210 Birch Street
Santa Paula, CA 93060
Beneficial insects

The Fertrell Company
PO Box 265
Bainbridge, PA 17502
Fertilizers, soil amendments

Francis Laboratories
1551 East Lafayette
Detroit, MI 48207
Natural fertilizers

Green Pro Services
380 S. Franklin Street
Hempstead, NY 11550
Natural gardening products

Growing Naturally
PO Box 54
149 Pine Lane
Pineville, PA 18946
Natural gardening products

Mellinger's
2310 W. South Range Road
Lima, OH 44452-9731
Fertilizers, soil conditioners, soil amendments

Natural Gardening Research Center
Highway 48
PO Box 149
Sunman, IN 47041
Beneficial insects, organic gardening supplies

Nitron Industries
4605 Johnson Road
PO Box 1447
Fayetteville, AR 72702
Natural fertilizers, soil enhancers

149

Ohio Earth Food, Inc.
13737 DuQuette Avenue NE
Hartville, OH 44632
*Natural gardening products,
specializing in sea products*

Reuter Labs, Inc.
8540 Natural Way
Manassas Park, VA 22111
Natural pest controls

Ricon-Vitove Insectaries
PO Box 475
Rialto, CA 92376
Beneficial insects

Ringer Corporation
9959 Valley View Road
Eden Prairie, MN 55344
*Soil amendments, irrigation
equipment, beneficial insects*

Safer, Inc.
60 William Street
Wellesley, MA 02181
*Pest controls, natural soaps,
natural herbicides*

INDEX

Illustrations are indicated by page numbers in *italics;*
charts and tables are indicated by page numbers in **bold.**

Water-Conserving Gardens and Landscapes

153

Index

Phosphorus, 34, 36, **38**
Photinia serrulata, 104, **123,** 140
Photosynthesis, 31, *32,* 33
Phyla nodiflora, 115, **129**
Phymotochrichum omnivorum, 137–140
Pine, 14, 99, **121**
Piñon pine, 105, **124**
Pinus spp., 14, 28, 99, 105, **121, 124**
Pistache, 41, 100, **121**
Pistacia spp., 41, 100, **121**
Plant
    diseases, 69, 90, 135, 137–140
    nutrition, 33–34
    pests, 37, **38–39,** 39–40, 56, 66, 133–137
    selection, 18, 44, 90–92, **93,** 94, **119**
    spacing, 18
    stress signs, 63–64
    structure, 32–33
Plant societies, 146–148
Planting times, 11, 90
Plastic sheeting, 29, 56, 66–67
Plumbago auriculata, 101–102, **122**
Plume grass, 113–114, **128**
Pogon spp., 109
Poinciana, 105, **124**
Pollination, 33
Polyethylene pipe tubing, 72–73
Polyethylene sheeting. *See* Plastic sheeting
Polypropylene landscape fabric, 66
Polyvinyl chloride pipe, 71
Pomegranate, 105, **124,** 140
Ponderosa pine, 99
Poppy, 92
Porous hardscapes, 21
Portulaca grandiflora, 109, 112, **127**
Potassium (Potash), 34, 36
Potato vine, 117, **130**
Potential hydrogen, 51–52
Potted plants. *See* Container plants
Pressure-compensating emit-

ters, 75
Pressure regulators, 77, 79, 82, *83*
Product suppliers, 146
Prosopis glandulosa torreyana, 40, 55, 104, **123**
Prunus spp., 104, **123**
Punica granatum, 105, **124**
Puya berteroniana, 109, **126**
PVC pipe, 71

Q
Quailbush, 106
Queen's-wreath, 15
Quercus spp., 98, **121**

R
Rain barrels, 65
Raised beds, 131–132
    and soil depth, 48, 55
    and water use, 11, 62, 85, 86
Redbud, 100, **121**
Red-leaved rose, 105
Red valerian, 109, **126**
Redwood dust, 67
Regional guide to plant selection, **93, 119–130**
Reservoirs, 65
Rhus spp., 100, **121**
Rice hulls, 66
Robinia spp., 98, **120**
Rockrose, 105, **124**
Romneya coulteri, 92, 109, **126**
Root
    depth, 48, *60,* 60–61
    hairs, 32
    irrigator, 70
    rot, **38,** 56, 137–140
Root growth
    encouraging, 11, 12, 48, 57
    and hardpan, 54
    inspection, 39–40
    and planting holes, 35
Rosa spp., 105, **124**
Rose, 105, **124,** 140
Rosemary, 16, 92, 105–106, 118, **124, 140**
Rose-moss, 109, 112, **127**
Rosmarinus spp., 16, 92, 105–106, **124**
Runoff, 69

Rustic landscape, 8
Ryegrass, 112

S
Sage, 92, 106, 118, **124**
Sagebrush, 101
St. Augustine grass, 112, **127**
St.-John's-bread, 95
Saline soil, 56–57
Salt buildup, **38,** 53–54, 56–57, 67
    in containers, 65, 132, 133
Saltbush, 106, **124**
Salvia spp., 92, 106, **124**
Sand mulch, 28–29, 66
Sand sage, 101
Sandy soil, 46, 47, 74, **76**
Santolina spp., 92, 115, **129**
Sawdust, 50, 52, 64, 66, 67
Schinus spp., 99, **121**
Sedum spp., 112, 115, **127, 129**
Seed
    inoculation, 36
    production, 33
    selection, 118
    suppliers, 145–146
Shade plants, 7, 13–14
Shallow-rooted plants, 74
She-oak, 94
Shore pine, 28
Shrubs, 94–107, **122–124**
Siberian elm, 96
Silk-tassel bush, 106, **124**
Silk tree, 100, **121**
Silt, 46, 47
Silverberry, 102, 140
Silver linden, 97–98
Silver princess, 96
Silver sage, 101
Sisyrinchium bellum, 107, **125**
Slick spot soil, 57
Smooth brome, 112, **127**
Snow-in-summer, 115, **129**
Soaker hoses, 70, 117–118
Soap sprays, 134
Soaptree, 107
Soapweed, 107
Soil
    acidic versus alkaline, 51–53

155

We'd love your thoughts…

Your reactions, criticisms, things you did or didn't like about this Storey Book. Please use space below (or write a letter if you'd prefer — even send photos!) telling how you've made use of the information . . . how you've put it to work . . . the more details the better! Thanks in advance for your help in building our library of good Storey Books.

M John Storey
Publisher

Book Title: _____

Purchased From: _____

Comments: _____

_____

_____

_____

_____

_____

Your Name: _____

Address: _____

☐ Please check here if you'd like our latest Storey's Books for Country Living Catalog.

☐ You have my permission to quote from my comments, and use these quotations in ads, brochures, mail, and other promotions used to market your books.

Signed _____ Date _____

SEPTEMBER 1992

From: _____